Priests

Priests

Images, Ideals, and Changing Roles

James A. Fischer

Foreword by Andrew M. Greeley

Dodd, Mead & Company • *New York*

Library of Congress Cataloging-in-Publication Data

Fischer, James A.
Priests: images, ideals, and changing roles.

Bibliography: p.
Includes index.
1. Pastoral theology—Catholic Church. 2. Catholic
Church—Clergy. 3. Priests. 4. Catholic Church—United
States—Clergy. I. Title.
BX1913.F475   1987   262'.142   87-15689
ISBN 0-396-08987-9

This book is dedicated to the Vatterott Family
in appreciation for the delightful days
I spent at their cabin at the Lake of
the Ozarks, where I wrote most of this book

—JAMES A. FISCHER

Contents

Acknowledgments   xi

Foreword by Andrew M. Greeley   xiii

Introduction   xix

ONE: The Fantasy of Father Smith   1

TWO: Historical Theology   19

    1. Introduction   21
       Paul, The Leader   22
    2. New Testament Times   27
       Ignatius of Antioch   29
       Augustine of Hippo   38
    3. The Era of the Fathers   44
       Thomas Aquinas   46
    4. The Medieval Order   53
       Charles Borromeo   54
    5. Reformation and Reform   58

THREE: Contemporary Problems   61

    1. A Survey of Official Statements   63
    2. Research Projects   67
    3. Theological Discussion   68
       Tim Dempsey, the Irish Priest   76
    4. The American Situation   81
       Father Tom, the Statistic   85
    5. Personal Problems of Priests   93

FOUR: Seminaries and the Future   99

       Joe Seminarian   101
    1. Introduction   106
    2. The Changes   107
    3. Problems   113
    4. The Prospects   115

FIVE: What Makes Father Run?   121

    1. Introduction   123
    2. A Brief History of Priestly Spirituality   124
    3. The Spirituality of American Seminaries   128
       Vincent de Paul   132
    4. The Vincentian Ideal of the Priest   141
    5. Going My Way?   145

SIX: The Nondistinctiveness of the Catholic Priest   149

1. Introduction   151
2. Vatican II and the Common Priesthood   154
3. The Spheres   156
4. The Priest and the Theologian   158
5. The Common Priesthood in the American Church   159
6. The Problem of How to Do It   161

SEVEN: Journey Into The Unknown   165

1. Where Is God?   167
2. The Priestly Office   170
3. The Paradoxes of the Priesthood   174

Final Note   177
Notes   181
Index   191

Acknowledgments

The author gratefully acknowledges the following publishers and authors for permission to quote from various books: Center for Applied Research in the Apostolate for citations from *Planning the Future;* Confraternity of Christian Doctrine for the biblical quotations from the *New American Bible;* Costello Publishing Co. for quotations from *Vatican Council II;* Fortress Press for a quotation from Bernard Cooke, *Ministry in Word and Sacraments: History and Theology;* Herder and Herder for the quote from Karl Rahner, *Servants of the Lord;* United States Catholic Conference for quotations from "Declaration on the Question of the Ordination of Women to the Ministerial Priesthood" and, Eugene F. Hemrick and Dean E. Hoge, *Seminarians in Theology: A National Profile;* Viking-Penguin for the excerpt from Graham Greene's, *The Power and the Glory;* and to Andrew M. Greeley for permission to cite from his books, *The Catholic Priest in the United States: Sociological Investigations; American Catholics since the Council: An Unauthorized Report* and *Ascent Into Hell.*

Photo credits are due to AP/Wide World Photos, Inc.; The Denver Catholic Register, Missouri Historical Society; Our Sunday Visitor, Huntington, Ind.; Sulpician Archives Baltimore; St. Mary's Seminary, Perryville, Mo. Archives; St. Thomas

Seminary Archives, Denver; and the artist Kathleen Rose for the pencil drawings.

I express my particular gratitude to Andrew M. Greeley for his graciousness in writing the preface and his permissions and encouragement. Especially I am indebted to my editor Mary Kennan of Dodd, Mead and Company who has always been capable of finding a way out of problems and smoothing the work. The book has had a long history; I am grateful to the faculty of Kenrick Seminary in St. Louis with whom this book began as a joint statement but has progressed to being a personal commentary. The good ideas are largely theirs.

James A. Fischer

Foreword

"The trouble," Blackie Ryan sighed, and *Letters of William James* slipped off his chest where it had been resting when I awakened him from his nap, "is that empiricists like you have no sense of the rhythms of history."

I had stopped by his room to tell the little monsignor that I was writing a Foreword to Jim Fischer's book on the priesthood. The "three Johns" of Blackie's adolescence (Kennedy, XXIII and Unitas) looked down on me from the wall, reminders of a better era. The saucy medieval ivory madonna and her even more saucy child watched me with their usual amusement.

"You're the follower of James and Whitehead, not me," I replied. "And Fischer uses Hugh Donlon and Sean Cronin in his book, but not you."

"My Lord Cronin will be pleased," he waved his small pudgy hand. "The perfect modern cardinal . . . but let me pursue my point. Am I not a reincarnation of G. K.'s Father Brown? And could you not have found priests like the two of us—

Father Brown and myself, I mean—at every point since the first bunch left Jerusalem? So why do you or the admirable Father Fischer trouble yourselves about the fads and fashions, the exposés and the infidelities, the alarums and the excursions of the present? And would you like a wee sip of Jameson's to ease the pain of your trip from Arizona? But of course, I have forgotten. You don't drink."

"The morale of the clergy is desperately low. Scandals are headline news. Recruitment is down. Rome is trying to undo the Vatican Council. Maybe we're finished."

Blackie struggled out of his vast easy chair, glanced out the window, noted it was snowing and zipped up his Chicago Bears jacket. "Tell me about it," he sighed again as he began to bustle about, making me raspberry tea to be served in the Belleek cups that his sisters give him. "What is the saying about the difference between England and Ireland? In the former the situation is always serious and never desperate, while in the latter it is always desperate but never serious?"

"The priesthood will survive the present crisis?" I demanded.

With some difficulty the little monsignor plugged his electric teakettle into a wall socket. "If you want odds on that," he glanced at me over his thick glasses, "I should say that they are of the same order of magnitude as that of the sun rising over Lake Michigan tomorrow morning."

"A crisis of growth, not decline?"

"As the admirable Noele Farrell says in another one of your little stories, 'Resurrection isn't supposed to be easy.' "

"Indeed."

"My line." He poured boiling water into the teapot. "How can we suppose that an institution like the priesthood, which has responded to human needs and challenges for fifteen hundred years, more or less, will phase itself out because of a few stories in the *National Catholic Reporter?*"

"Okay, but it's tough to be a priest these days. So many crises of confidence and identity."

"What is it that the playwright says?" He examined the teapot and shook his head in bafflement. "Mediocrity is not an option. 'Thank God our times are now. The enterprise is exploration into God.' For a thousand years at least, they'll envy us the privilege of renewing the priesthood."

"So what should I tell them in the Foreword to Jim's book?"

"So tell them," he beamed as the tea, astonishingly, came out of the spout of the teapot, "that one of the signs of hope is that men like Jim are writing such sensitive and intelligent books about the present crisis."

"True enough," I admitted.

"Also, tell Jim to put me in the next book, and possibly the inestimable Father Ace McNamara, and perhaps my fellow papal broom-sweeper, Packy Keenan." He smiled happily as if the feat of offering me a teacup was nearly miraculous. "And that the God who made such a delight as raspberry tea—and tea and raspberries separately considered—is not likely to let us down. Even if sometimes She must find our faintness of heart discouraging."

"I see."

"Like Jesus," he looked for his own teacup, a hint of suspicion in his baffled frown that a demon, or perhaps a golem, had stolen it, "in the storm on the Sea of Galilee. 'Save us, Lord, lest we perish!' "

"Indeed," we both said together.

The saucy madonna seemed to be grinning. Her kid, too.

—ANDREW M. GREELEY

The priests asked not,
"Where is the LORD?"

—JEREMIAH 2:8

Introduction

This book is about Catholic priests. It picks up the threads of history interwoven with contemporaneity to describe the priesthood as it is today. The problems and possibilities confronting this ancient institution arise from the past more than is true with almost any other group; the future is both more predictable and less.

The ideas behind the priesthood have not been formed in a vacuum; there is no history of ideas, only of people. The beliefs of the people crucial to the development of the priesthood came from the stress and crunch of life at critical times. So also what priests think themselves to be today, and what people accept or reject them for, is not a matter of abstract theology. It is a matter of concrete realities; most of all, it is a matter of images.

This book was planned as a theological study by a seminary faculty. As it progressed, however, it became clear that the images were more important than the academic theology. Also, our students were more important to us than were the theories. The present author decided to abandon the completely academic format and approach the subject by way of vignettes about key persons in the history. The stories begin with a fantasy about media images of priests which allows the contemporary problems to jostle one another. The story telling approach allows only a sampling of the wealth of priest lore, but it is hoped that the selection is sufficiently broad to capture the principal ideas. The story form relies on authentic information, although some imaginary dialogue has had to be created from it. Between the chapters are brief reflections on what the author sees as the theological significance. Then follows the research data and the theological investigations. Amid the stories you will find the facts and theories of contemporary discussion.

As an author, I hope that I may communicate to you, the reader, something of the excitement and drama that are involved. I cannot promise objectivity—nobody can. I can only assure you that the book has been researched to the limit of my ability. The final outcome is a "journey into the unknown."

—JAMES A. FISCHER

Priests

ONE

The Fantasy of Father Smith

Father Smith was about to doze off, the novel open on the desk before him. He knew that he should not have been wasting his time reading another priest story, but he found it irresistible. In his half-asleep state he dreamed that the devil was tempting him. As his head sank, his nose was literally in the book and it seemed to him that the devil was rubbing it in. He could feel the cream-colored paper abrading the tip of his nose. The rubbing continued and soon his whole nose was in the page; then his face, his head, his shoulders, the rest of his torso. With a final push on his legs, he completely disappeared into the book and all that was left of him was a dark smudge on the page. The devil took out a handkerchief and fastidiously dusted away the last sign of Father Jules Smith.

Inside the page, Father Smith struggled to his feet and looked around. He seemed to be in a narrow corridor made of an attractively translucent material that extended far above his head and curved gently at the top where the page had begun to curl. There were dark spots on the walls of the corridor; he assumed the spots were printed words, although he could not make them out. The corridor came to an abrupt turn and continued on, one wall now darker than the other, but each seemingly without end. Then the whole corridor suddenly trembled, and Father Smith fell flat on the floor as it seemed to hinge around and circle. He felt a jerk as it came to rest again, and now the dark side of the corridor was on the left-hand side. Some minutes passed as he reoriented himself. He did not seem to be the worse for wear, and slowly he rose to his feet. That was when he spotted Pam Schiller. Pam was the local religion reporter for the daily paper; she was also a parishioner, a fact that she tried to conceal in her professional life.

"Well, hello, Pam," he said in surprise. "What are you doing here?"

"Same as you," she replied. "Looking for a story."

"That's business with you. I'm just here on pleasure."

"Is that so?" Pam retorted in her standard reportorial voice. "You make your living by telling stories."

"Ah, well," he winked. "Just don't quote me as saying that."

As he became accustomed to this strange situation, he heard a crackling sound and the right-hand wall of the corridor darkened as another page was turned. Down at the far end, where the spine of the book would be, Father Smith saw a bit of light shining into the corridor and he headed toward it.

The door was ajar and he could see into an impressive-looking office. As he pushed the door open, the man behind the mahogany desk called out, "Come in, Father Smith. We have been waiting for you."

Smith entered and found that the office conformed to his first impression. It was somber, paneled in a dark wood. A subdued rug lay on the floor and several lamps were burning, as well as the fluorescent ceiling lights. The man behind the desk was dressed as a priest. Sitting in a chair in front of the desk was a distinguished-looking, middle-aged gentleman with silver hair, a ruddy face and an eager expression.

"Well, Jules," said this man, "good to see you in the flesh. You know Cardinal Cronin here. Call him Sean."

"And this," said the cardinal, "is Hugh Donlon."

"Donlon," Smith mused. "I must know you from somewhere."

"You met me in a book," Hugh told him. "Andy Greeley's *Ascent Into Hell*. I was the bad actor. Just out of a federal correction institution for violating the Commodities Futures Trading Act. Acquitted. And now this man is trying to persuade me to do the noble thing and come back to the priesthood."

"No, that's not so," said the cardinal. "All I am saying is that no matter what you do, you're a priest of this archdiocese, and never forget it."

"It's been so hard to know . . ." Hugh stammered. "Should I have been a priest in the first place? Should I have left? Should I return now?"

"Why can't you have a vocation in the active ministry for a while and then take on a different vocation? I want you back, Hugh, but only if you're convinced it's the best way for you to go. Either way, you're a priest. The choice is between active ministry or being a priest in some other way no one has yet quite figured out—representing the church and, yes, ministering for the church in whatever world you're in."

"I think I need more time."

"Wait a minute, Hugh," Father Smith put in. "That's a magnanimous offer. Too damn magnanimous, if you want my opinion, cardinal or no cardinal. Who's trying to manipulate who around here?"

The cardinal glared at Jules.

"You're making him an offer that you know you can't back up in Rome," Jules pointed out. "You're being magnanimous about his supposed freedom and offering it to him free of charge. Who'd want a priest like that?"

"Oh, come off the legalisms, Jules," Hugh put in. "We're talking about people, not rules. And you know I won't come back unless I want to."

"That's what I am talking about—people. Is the church only concerned about another do-gooder who wants to save the world? In whose name are you offering people salvation?"

"I don't know, and that's my problem, not yours," Hugh retorted.

"Oh, isn't it?" Jules blurted out. "I've read all those novels about the hero priest who left for some higher good than he could find in this crummy church, and how out there in the realm of pure love he can finally bring God to everybody."

"That's not so, Jules. I haven't brought much love to anybody. But I don't know if I would be a bigger fraud by coming back or by staying where I am."

For some reason, Pam seemed to become visible at that moment. "What in the world are you men talking about? All this palaver about sacred trusts and high principles. Let him make up his mind one way or the other and get it over with."

"Hmm, well," the cardinal said, looking at his watch, "I have to run. Nice meeting you, Jules. We don't see people like you every day."

He shook hands all around and departed. Father Smith made his own farewells and found himself out in the high corridor once again. He hadn't understood it all very well, but then his memory for the details in the book was growing dull. He confessed to himself that perhaps he had been a bit hasty and that he didn't really fit into this kind of scene. After all, he was from a lost generation. Or was he?

As he wandered down the high corridor, he came to quite a different kind of room. This was a miserable prison cell. A little man was huddled in one corner and a tall soldier, his hand on his revolver, stood over the cringing figure. There was no doubt as to who this was. Even in the odoriferous place, one smell dominated. This was the Whiskey Priest, Padre Juan.

Graham Greene had put him in this cell in *The Power and the Glory*, and here he would remain, forever incarcerated in literature.

"We have to die sometime," the lieutenant was saying. "It doesn't seem to matter so much when."

"You're a good man. You've nothing to be afraid of."

"You have such odd ideas," the lieutenant complained, adding, "sometimes I feel you're just trying to talk me round."

"Round to what?"

"Oh, to letting you escape perhaps, or to believing in the holy Catholic Church, in the communion of saints . . . how does that stuff go?"

"The forgiveness of sins."

"You don't believe much in that, do you?"

"Oh, yes, I believe," the little man said obstinately.

"Then what are you worried about?"

"I'm not ignorant, you see. I've always known what I've been doing. And I can't absolve myself."

"Would Padre Jose's coming here have made all that difference?"

He had to wait a long while for his answer, and then he didn't understand it when it came: "Another man . . . it makes it easier."

"Is there nothing more I can do for you?"

"No. Nothing."

The lieutenant opened the door, mechanically putting his hand again upon his revolver; he felt moody, as though now that the last priest was under lock and key, there was nothing left to think about. The spring of action seemed to be broken. He looked back on the weeks of hunting his quarry as a happy time, over now forever. He felt without a purpose, as if life had drained out of the world.

Father Smith entered the cell, sat down on a bench and looked for a long time at the miserable, crouching creature before him.

"Would you have done it all over?" he asked.

"Done what?" Padre Juan countered. "Gotten drunk? Neglected my duties? Said my Masses without a thought except to get through? No, I'm not proud of all that, nor will I defend it. It was wrong, and I must live and die with it."

"I don't mean that," said Jules. "I mean, would you have been a priest at all had you known how it would turn out?"

"That's an impossible question," the prisoner said. "Nobody can answer that. You can answer that only by a life. Do I regret being a priest? No, that's the one dignity I had. Being a recalcitrant priest and refusing to marry—although I fathered a child—no, I am not sorry about that."

"What's the purpose of it all?" Jules asked.

"Purpose? Who knows the purpose until it's over? I knew I had to baptize and absolve and say Mass even at my worst times. They needed it. I was the one appointed. Why, I don't know. But that's how it was."

"I don't understand that," Jules said.

"Of course you don't," the Whiskey Priest replied. "You sit in your rectory and read books. You don't have to face the guns. And yet there is something in you too that says it must be done."

"Well, I suppose I believe that, but it seems such a fragile conclusion."

"Faith, my friend, is a terrible thing. It can't be explained but it forces us to such desperate choices."

Jules shook his head. He had always thought that faith was rather comforting; at least he had said so—perhaps pretended to believe so—in all those sermons he had given. Faith as terror was something different.

As he stood up and was about to leave the tiny cell, Padre Juan said, "Thank you for coming. I am afraid that my creator has left me to die. You are a good man."

"Well," Pam Schiller murmured, mostly to herself, as they left, "that was puzzling. What's the answer?"

"Pam," he said, "even the *Daily Tribune* knows better than to ask that."

The corridor still stretched on. Father Smith pursued his way until he found a substantial door with a red warning light blinking above it. As he pushed open the door, he could hear a boys' choir singing something about "if you want to be a pig. . . ." Almost before he entered the room, which seemed to be a studio, a gruff voice said, "Hey, you, you can't come in here."

But Father Smith took time for a quick look around. "Isn't that Bing Crosby?" he asked. "And isn't this the set for *Going My Way?*"

"You're not allowed in here," the security guard said. "We've been chasing guys like you out of here for ages. Why do you persist in coming back?"

Father Smith took a somewhat longer look at the set. It surely was *Going My Way*. But there was a huge truck with monstrous sucking pipes parked near it, and men shielded in white coveralls and masks were going about their business. On one side of the truck in flamboyant letters was printed: Detoxification Unit. "What's that truck doing over there?"

"You can read, can't you, bub?" the security guard said. "We've been trying for years to clean up this mess. You get this stuff into the atmosphere and it's practically impossible to get it out again."

"Why do you want to get it out?"

"Orders straight from the top," the guard replied. "Come on now. Out you go." He whipped out an instrument with a digital readout and moved it over Father Smith's clothing. "Yeah, you've got some of it on you already. That's about all we allow for one day. So let's get moving."

As they left, Pam Schiller was laughing. "Well, if you wanted fiction, that was it."

"I'm not so sure it was all fiction," Father Smith replied.

As they reentered the corridor, he saw a similar door on

the other side and hoped that he would receive a better reception than the last. And indeed he did. As he pushed the door open, a smiling, florid-faced man in striking sports clothes came rushing up to greet him. "Welcome, welcome, Father Smith," he gushed. "We were waiting for you. Come and meet some of the others. Brother Alexis, come here. Put down those copies and let the Xerox machine alone. Meet Father Smith. He's from the other world."

Brother Alexis beamed with kindness and exuded simplicity. "Oh, Father," he said, "you're just a carbon copy, if I may put it that way, of what I always imagined a priest to be. Come and meet some of the other characters. Here's Sister Genevieve, the Blue Nun. And here's Father Jones, busy polishing the Chrysler for our next commercial. They will all be glad to see you. Can we get you a special discount or something?"

"Here, here," said the sporty host, "let me fix up your appearance. Take off that smoking jacket and put on this clerical collar and coat. Can't go on the air without the proper credentials, can we? And the frown. We'll have to do away with that, won't we? Or maybe not. How about this ice cream? Would you just have a little and say, 'This Heavenly Hash is positively sinful'? That would be just right. I'm sure you would go over big with the public. Give a little authenticity to our games here. And there will be a nice stipend for it." Clapping his hands, he cried out in a loud voice, "Stipend! Stipend!"

All that Father Smith could think to do was to shout, "Forty days and Nineveh will be destroyed!"

"Here, here," said the gusher. "None of that around here. That's not nice. On TV you have to be nice or you're not going to sell anything. Give them a little security and pat them on the head a bit. That's what they want. Let them know that you're just like them, only better. Maybe it would be better yet if you were a bishop. Hey, Joe," he yelled, "one bishop front and center."

"Try a woman priest," Pam said suddenly.

"Lady, what are you, some kind of radical? You can't sell anything with a priest in high heels. You've got to back it up with tradition," the gusher said.

Father Smith was innocent of ecclesiastical ambitions. He quickly found the door and slammed it behind him, still holding a spoonful of ice cream.

"Tradition!" Pam exploded. "That's the answer for everything."

"I suppose it is," Father Smith said.

"And so you beat down women with your traditions while you're the very ones who keep making up the traditions. All those old men in Rome who decide what's best for us!"

"You want to be a priest?" Father Smith asked.

"Not on your life," Pam replied. "I'm happy with my job, and I make a lot more money than you do."

"At least the second part is true. But why be so excited about something you don't want?"

"I know some women who do want to be priests. They're willing to give their all, and they feel left out. They could be a tremendous advantage . . . or do only men understand religion? Every other church gives women their equal place, but this out-of-step Catholic Church keeps saying that since Christ was a male, women are forever barred. Isn't the Holy Spirit telling us something today?"

"I'm sure the Holy Spirit is telling us a lot today, but I don't know for sure what it is. And it's certainly not simply male prejudice that's involved," Father Smith said as he absently slipped the spoon into his jacket pocket. "I wish it were. I could repent and you could forgive me." He smiled at her and she winked back: You're not so bad after all.

Farther down the corridor they came upon an academic-looking door marked: Eng. 107. Father Smith quietly opened it and they found themselves looking into a large lecture room, obviously at a university. He found a chair toward the back and sat down to watch the proceedings.

"Who's he?" he whispered to the student beside him.

"Tuffly Riddle," the student whispered back. "Great stuff about the novel. I'm going to write one, that's why I'm here. The Third."

"Third novel?" asked Father Smith, incredulous.

"No, Riddle. Tuffly Riddle the Third."

"Oh," said Father Smith, as though he understood why this was important.

"X," said Professor Riddle dramatically, and he put a large X on the blackboard. "That's what it's all about."

"What's he talking about?" Father Smith inquired.

"We're on priest novels today," the would-be novelist told him. "Listen, will you? Be quiet."

Professor Riddle was obviously well in stride now. "The sub-genre of the clerical novel has had a great history, from Chaucer's *Canterbury Tales* to Colleen McCullough's *The Thorn Birds*, if I dare mention them both in the same breath. And we can toss in everything in between, which would make a considerable catalog. I don't intend to consider it."

"How about O'Donovan and *The Rosary Murders*, or G. K. Chesterton and the Father Brown Stories?" a neophyte from the drugstore library called out.

"I would not deign to render an opinion on such supposed mystery stories," the professor sighed. "Basically, there are only two kinds of priest books. One deals with the priest who fails. That is exceedingly difficult to write about well. The other deals with the priest who succeeds. That kind is impossible. At least it is impossible for the reader."

"Who wants to read about priests anyway?" someone else called out.

"The public," replied the professor curtly.

"Hell, all priests ever do is preach about doing good in the most uncomfortable way possible. Or being roasted, which at least is more exciting."

"Ah, my young genius, you haven't caught on yet," said the professor, and he turned his back to contemplate his X.

"As Laurence Sterne once said, all good stories are based on emotions that go astray and run into conflict. At least Sterne said something like that. Look it up if you want the proper quotation. You can tell that kind of story about any two or more human beings. The value of the story depends on how authentically you describe the emotions and how well you understand the conflict."

"So why make a big deal out of priests?" another student asked.

"Because of X. X is the uncontrolled force, the mystery factor. Part of it, you might say, is community expectation. Television commercials use priests and monks and nuns because they are instantly identifiable with certain values the public either thinks it embraces or wishes it could. But the people who have to live with these values take a different view of them."

He went on: "You can make an excellent story about a broken marriage. If you do a good job, you have something more than sex and affection to deal with. You have a haunting suspicion of something sacred that lies beyond the human emotions. But when you deal with priests, you know that there is an X. If you throw in sex, it is not simply spice for the tale. Adultery is not just 'Stolen water is sweet, and bread gotten secretly is pleasing,' as Proverbs gently put it so many centuries ago. Betrayal is the name of the game, and betrayal is of an absolute. Don't ask me what the absolute is. Years ago the story was often told of a priest who fell away from his vows and wanted to come back. But he had to ask Rome for permission, and every time he did, the answer was always: *Pereat!* At least so the stories went. 'Let him perish!' There is a satisfying absolute in that. It may never have happened, and of course there were always ways around it. But the threat was there. And that is life."

"I don't believe all that nonsense; just tell the story," a skeptical adolescent said.

"Ah, but you do want to hear the story," the professor rejoined. "You wouldn't reject it so crassly if it didn't pique your interest."

"Father Smith," he went on, "you can tell us about this. Why are you a priest anyway?"

"I don't know," Father Smith answered. "I just have to be."

"Do you like it?"

"Yes and no. I like helping people. I don't like myself too much. I suppose that I should be 'the Wounded Healer,' the man who accepts his own weakness and out of that tries to help others. But that doesn't really work very well, except for a while as a clever ploy. It's difficult to preach when one has to listen. You people can turn me off when I speak. I can't."

"Don't you believe what you say?"

"That's my curse. I do believe. My other curse is that I don't."

"Can you explain that?"

"X," said Father Smith.

"Well," Professor Riddle said, turning away, "that's all for today. Tomorrow we will consider comedy . . . unless you believe that that's what we were talking about today."

As they came out of the room, Pam looked thoughtful. "Is that really all you have to go on?" she asked.

"Oh, yes," Father Smith replied. "It's a matter of faith, and one walks by faith, not by light, you know."

The corridor stretched on once more. As they went along, Father Smith could feel the wall on the right growing warm and the one on the left cooling down. At the end of the corridor, which now became visible, he could see a small foyer. As he neared it, he heard shrieks and hideous grinding noises coming from the right, and the wall had become unbearably hot. When he stopped and put his ear to the left wall, he could hear the pleasant sounds of a waterfall, and birds singing. He had finally come to a cul-de-sac and as he entered it, he heard a door quietly slide closed behind him, and Pam Schiller vanished from view. He was trapped, all alone.

Then he noticed that there were three doors in the foyer. On the right there was an iron door that seemed to be almost incandescent. On it was written one word: *Pereat!* But what lay behind it one never knew, for as he studied it, the dire sounds seemed to come from every direction. The door on the left was impressively decorated with a coat of arms, with the physician's caduceus worked into it. Underneath was written: The Wounded Healer. He could hear the idyllic sounds of a springtime forest behind it. Or were they behind it? The third door was almost invisible. It blended into the rest of the foyer; nothing was written on it and nothing in the nature of a promise or a threat seemingly lay behind it.

Father Smith pondered all three doors. Obviously he had to go through one of them if he were to return to the living world. Yet each presented a mystery and a threat. Were the sounds symbolic of what lay beyond each door? Or were they a deception? And what was the third door all about? He was afraid of *Pereat!* and distrustful of The Wounded Healer. Slowly he reached out his hand, took the knob of the third door and twisted it.

As he did so, a loud bell rang. With a start, Father Smith awoke to stare at the telephone beside him on the desk. He picked up the receiver and was instantly in touch with the real world in the person of Pat McLaughlin, chairman of the parish council.

"When are you going to get over here for this meeting?" Pat was demanding indignantly.

And so Father Smith never knew which door he had really gone through.

Priest Novels

I am indebted to Andrew W. Greeley for brief quotations from *Ascent Into Hell* (New York: Warner Books, 1983), and to Graham Greene, *The Power and the Glory* (New York: Time, Inc., 1940). The classroom scene is somewhat cribbed from an excellent article by James E. Johnston, "Priests, Prose and Preachment," in *Theology Today,* 41 (1984), 161–171.

REFLECTIONS

The bit of whimsy in this chapter is simply intended to give point to the fact that the concept of the Roman Catholic priesthood is dependent on images and that these images cause the problems. This is true whether one is talking about contemporary popular views or academic historical views. I shall attempt to illustrate the latter in subsequent chapters.

Within this view of priests there is an X factor. If you are somewhat surprised that I pictured Father Smith as a bit uncertain of the nature of the X factor but firmly convinced of its reality, my reply is that to me this reflects the attitude of the actual men whom I shall describe later. The X factor lies somewhere on the boundary between knowing what a priest *does* and what a priest *is.* The doing has constantly changed in the course of history and is changing right now, which is why *Going My Way* no longer approximates the current model. The contemporary emphasis is on functions; yet in popular imagery there is still something in the man that makes a priest clearly recognizable. The outreach from within toward something that is absolute and different clothes him much more than does his clerical garb.

The crucial point expressed here is that both aspects—function and nature—are stated in images. A priest cannot be described without the use of certain concrete delineations. Primarily these concern his actions. But it is also true that most of the abstract definitions are expressed in images as well: "another Christ," "dispenser of mysteries," "sacrifice and sacrificer," or even the modern terms, "Wounded Healer," "servant leader" and "community shepherd."

Relatively little about priesthood has actually been defined in the way that Catholics consider "defined faith." The Council of Trent in 1563 made most of the statements, but they must be considered within their time frame and the academic imagery in which they were expressed. A large store of theological opinion prevailing up to Vatican II described priesthood in considerable detail. This has a value that cannot be easily ignored, and it often appears in official documents. However, it is not defined faith.

On the other hand, there is much in the popular imagination of Catholicism that "defines" priesthood more realistically. Part of it is peripheral; after all, Christ did not wear a Roman collar. And yet the populace senses that there is something substantial that fits a man to be a priest within a worshiping community. Catholicism without priesthood is unthinkable. Although we speak of a priesthood of all the baptized, we always quickly add that there is a difference between the ministerial priesthood and the priesthood of the laity. What that precise difference is, we are finding more difficult to say. It is not just that certain people do things that others do not. Nor does "ministerial priesthood" mean simply professionalism, as though the difference lay between the professionals and the amateurs. It is quite evident in our church that sometimes the amateurs are more adept than the professionals.

A phrase in use since the Middle Ages speaks of *ex opere operato,* which is almost untranslatable but means that the priestly effect comes from that which is done by the priest, not from his personal competence. The phrase further has something to do with "character" (however it may be defined), meaning not the personal integrity of the minister, but the enduring change within him. There is also the leadership that transcends personal charism or managerial skill. Graham Greene illustrated something of this in his unhappy hero, Padre Juan.

The aim of the following chapters will be to illustrate certain essential ideas of the priesthood by studying them in the imaged circumstances of their crucial moment of growth in the history. The academic theology will be interspersed with stories;

it always has been. While the convictions reflect human needs and human deeds, they have come out of the hard realism of the times, often squeezed through the orifice of conflict and disaster. They are limited, sometimes almost misshapen, and they need at a later time to be homogenized into the whole mix. But they represent the reality of lifesaving images that we could not have done without.

TWO

Historical
Theology

1. Introduction

The history of ideas about the priesthood is really a history of people. The discipline of historical theology is always in danger of separating the "story" from the "history". The stories which I will use will try to make theological ideas part of living tissue. No one in the long tradition of the Catholic priesthood was an abstraction; each person was an individual with his own story, which governed what he wrote and did and why it was accepted. The same is true of those who write theology in our own times. Jean Galot and Edward Schillebeeckx differ today on their evaluations and projections for the priesthood not so much because they deal with different facts or use different logic, but because they have different stories to tell.[1] So also does the author.

However, at this point, as we examine a few stories, it may be helpful to try to put together the generally known facts about the historical development, if so it may be called. It would be presumptuous to pretend that this will be an in-depth study; all that is intended here is to align the stories' principal images with the historical theology.[2]

The stories are about tough men, men with strong views on authority and priesthood. Yet they were men who doubted. This was true of Paul, Ignatius and Augustine, of Thomas Aquinas and Tim Dempsey, as well as of our typical contemporaries. Vincent de Paul, after long years of working to establish seminaries in France, said he was certain that the church would never fail but he was not sure that the church in France would survive. These men lived with crises in their society; their leadership came not from abstract theorizing but from meeting critical situations head on. Change usually came about because social conditions changed.

Yet change in society does not usually take place in a clearly plotted line like that of an aircraft guided to a landing by radar. Change is sporadic. It starts, stops and then starts up again someplace else. We never lose the pieces of the past, but neither do we ever seem to put them all together. The establishment always has more power to resist than logic would suppose; the revolution runs out of steam sooner than the enthusiasts expect. The revolution that comes after the revolution is usually the one that remains, if it remains at all.

PAUL, THE LEADER

"Pay the bill, Priscilla," Paul said.

"But Paul, this is the second time in six months that Tyrannus has raised the rent for the lecture hall," she said.

"That's not unusual," he told her. "You and Aquila know that better than I do since you are always making deals with these people."

Priscilla could not help smiling at this impetuous man who

so openly and unashamedly used them. He did have a lot to do, and they were glad to be involved. They had come to Ephesus especially to bring him news from Corinth. That was before Stephanas, Fortunatus and Achaicus had arrived with even more pressing business. Paul had the reports before him now, which was why he was not interested in something as banal as rent. He shuffled the manuscripts and looked at her with a smile.

"What about Apollos?" he asked. "You knew him better than I. I met him for only a few days here. What did you really think of him?"

"Honest. Intelligent. Somewhat naive," she answered without hesitancy.

"Naive, eh?" He seemed interested. "What gave you that idea?"

"Well, he had all those fine philosophical explanations about the Way before he even knew much about Jesus. And he was baptizing before he knew that there was something more than the baptism of John."

"Causing real trouble?"

"Oh, I don't think so. We both know those Corinthian business types, and I don't think they will be all that enthusiastic. The bigger difficulty is with those other ones, the dock-workers and the street-cleaners and the maids and those poorer people who have come over to us. They get their heads in the sky too easily."

Paul chuckled. "Promise them wisdom and they'll be yours for life. There is a thrill to it. I remember when I was younger and studying in Jerusalem, we came to Proverbs and I was taken in completely by those soaring thoughts about Lady Wisdom. God seemed so close that you couldn't get him out of the earth, and then again, everything seemed turned into God. Then I met Jesus and I knew what Wisdom meant. It's rather too much all of a sudden. I too would think I knew all mysteries if I hadn't had to learn that wisdom doesn't come that easily."

"So what are you going to tell them?" she asked.

"Well, we need to stop this silly running after names. But that's not the true problem. Wisdom is. It's real . . . and yet it's a mystery. I'll have to tell them that from my own experience; otherwise they won't believe it."

He went back to reading the reports in front of him. "Tell me what you know about these disturbances during the Lord's Supper," he said.

"Well," Priscilla answered, "they didn't amount to much. We were still meeting in Stephanas's house next to the synagogue. You remember that he had that large parlor and that we could overflow into the courtyard if we needed to. That fat fellow was there, Domitillus I think his name is, who always had his slave come with two chairs, he was so huge. And then there would be a commotion when he pushed enough people away to set up his chairs. He always looked like he wanted to be a king. And he would preside grandly and have his slave hand out bread and meat and wine."

"That's what they say is the trouble. Apparently the rest of them are feeling pressured to outdo that fellow and it's becoming more of a banquet than a remembrance and celebration of the Lord's Supper. They just haven't been given sufficient instruction yet." He paused and looked thoughtful. "What about those women we had trouble keeping quiet?"

Priscilla laughed. "Women will be women," she said. "They were always chattering anyway. When they found that they were talking in tongues, they just couldn't resist."

"Sounded like a madhouse," he mused. "The men were just as bad. If some of our pagan friends had come in, they would have thought we were all crazy. We are going to have to put a stop to that. Let them talk in order, and briefly."

"You will be the great one if you can do that," Priscilla said. "You taught them to expect the Holy Spirit to talk through them and now you want to put a lid on it."

"We have to," Paul said. "I know that all of them are enthusiastic; there are no better people anywhere. And they must have freedom; that's what we're all about. But we also need order, and I am the one responsible for seeing that things don't get out of hand."

"Paul, freedom is a heady item, and you may have gone too far."

He smiled and said, "I have been told that before, Prisca."

He pulled over a page of papyrus and began to write. Then he read the words aloud: " 'Men should regard us as servants of Christ and administrators of the mysteries of God.' That's the first point. After that we will get to these other problems. Tell Aquila that I would like to talk to you and him this evening. And get Sosthenes. Let's see if we can begin to write a letter to those people in Corinth."

Bibliography

The above dialogue is based broadly on the text of the First Letter to the Corinthians. The picture of Paul depends on my own research and, of course, I would not expect any consensus about Paul. However, it is interesting to note that Hans Conzelmann, *I Corinthians* (Philadelphia: Fortress, 1975), also places great stress on Paul's control of the liturgical life of the Corinthian community. For background details, see commentaries of William F. Orr and James Arthur Walther, *I Corinthians* (AB, Garden City, N.Y.: Doubleday, 1976).

REFLECTIONS

Paul never referred to himself as a priest. The word in our contemporary sense is not used in Paul's writings. He called himself an "apostle," one sent to preach the Gospel, which sometimes he referred to as "my Gospel."

However, there are certain things connected with priestly existence and activity in his writings, and they are important both in themselves and for our purposes. The first was his authority. He was an "apostle of Jesus Christ," commissioned by God. He was commissioned to preach not only the stories that were told of Jesus and that appear in the Gospels—his writings antedate them—but he was called to preach the meaning of these events in terms of what had happened to one who was the very model of a human being, an image of man as well as an image of God. The final confession, "Christ has died, Christ has risen," was not only a statement of historical fact, but a proclamation of what human life was all about and how it could be lived.

The difficulties uncovered in the First Letter to the Corinthians center around two experienced facts: freedom and enthusiasm. The Corinthians had not only "been converted"; they had experienced for the first time in their lives freedom from the constraints and limitations of paganism. Life was no longer limited to the docks where they worked, the hovels where they lived ("Not many of you are wise, as men account wisdom; not many are influential; and surely not many are well-born" [1 Corinthians 1:26]), the endless rounds of senseless and diverting merriment that pagan religious celebrations offered on a scheduled basis. They had discovered that they were sons of God and that they had a limitless future, as Jesus himself lived a glorified life. Death had been conquered. They were free.

And they were enthusiastic about it. With Paul's coming, there had begun to happen all those surprising events that lifted people out of themselves: the miraculous healings, the unwonted concern for others, the speaking in tongues, as examples. Paul had promised this freedom and it had arrived. Enthusiasm was the order of the day.

Heady stuff. But freedom, of course, soon got out of hand. Moral constraint either vanished or was interpreted in odd ways. Enthusiasm became a contest for seeing who could produce the most startling effects. "The Way" was in danger of becoming another PR business, with success assured by competing companies.

Paul used authority. He began by denouncing the rivalry of the factions that had appeared in Corinth. As a young man, he himself had experienced the thrill of discovering the wisdom within his own Jewish tradition, a wisdom wedding God so close to earth that at times it was impossible to distinguish the earthly from the divine or to confine the appearances within the divinity. Paul could understand the Corinthians, who had always wanted to be considered sophisticated savants, confident of finding their wisdom without schooling or effort. Their desire was not wrong; their way of going about it was. Paul disclaimed any philosophical pretenses; he presented himself as a plain, blunt-spoken man who talked of crucifixion and suffering. The Corinthians must act in like manner. He laid his authority for these statements on the line. He was an apostle; they were children. He was truly an ambassador, commissioned to treat of the mysteries, and he left little doubt about how it was to be done.

Having asserted this authority, Paul went on to exert it in other ways. He had opinions on what women should wear on their heads, on how people were to conduct themselves at civic festivals, on how they were to dress and eat and stand during the celebration of the Lord's Supper, on who was to speak in church, and in what order. He did not refer to himself as a priest, and he did not mention any sacramental acts—except to allude half-apologetically to the fact that he had baptized a few people—but he clearly had a concern for what was later called sacramental celebration, and he thought that he had the authority to do something about it. In fact, his claim to authority is sometimes rather embarrassing.

2. New Testament Times

The Gospel picture of Jesus begins by casting him in the role of rabbi. The first stories of him show him as a teacher who assembled learners ("disciples") around himself. At times he sent these disciples out to teach. Among them a distinct group slowly came to be identified as the "Apostles," the "sent ones." The distinction is not always clear in the New Testament texts, but the event of enumerating twelve Apostles is (cf. Matthew

10:2 ff., and parallels, and Acts I:26). To these persons Jesus seems to have given distinctive powers, notably those of forgiving sins and celebrating the memorial of his last supper.

Then the strange events of his life began to overtake him and he was done in by his enemies, crucified and raised from the dead. While the teaching phase had its own built-in explanations to a certain extent, the events of his last days stood in greater need of interpretation. The interpretation always centered around the significance of the passion, death and resurrection as redemptive, although it and its consequences were shaped differently by the different Gospels. The only incident that seems to unite the two phases was that of the Last Supper scene, in which he inaugurated a meal that was to be repeated— clearly for its redemptive value, as the texts say. In that way, the Old Testament became linked to the New and provided for continual access to God.

The Pauline literature, which antedates the written Gospels, is more professedly interpretative of the events of the life of Jesus. Here the nature of the man, the redemptive nature of his life and our connection with it through a church and its essential worship act, are much stronger and deeper. It is an interpretation that emphasizes the need for communion with Jesus by faith and with one another in loving service. As an Apostle, Paul had no doubt about his authority to shape both the liturgical and the service lives of his churches. The correspondence to the churches leaves no question about that. Charismatic ministry within his churches was held on a tight rein, or at least he tried to keep it so.

The emergence of some kind of organization centered around teaching authority and redemptive liturgical acts is evident in the later strata of New Testament writing, especially in the so-called Pastoral Epistles. There are differentiations of people both within some charismatic order and within some organizational structure, and sometimes they mingle. The church of the New Testament was not entirely charismatic, nor entirely sacramental, nor entirely organizational, to use terms we later created. In fact, the emerging shape of the community slowly gave a whole new meaning to the common but not religious word, "church."

The word "priest" and its contemporary connotations are not used in the New Testament. It appears in the Epistle to the Hebrews, and there it refers exclusively to Christ the High Priest and his eternal mediatorial role. All the baptized relate to him as the one mediator in the same way. Although Hebrews does not treat of an order of priests, some of the Old Testament imagery undoubtedly affected the later descriptions of those who came to be called priests or bishops.[3]

The terms "bishop," "presbyter" and "deacon" appear in the New Testament but without precise definitions; other words for services and practitioners also appear. Bishops are leaders of some sort; presbyters are primarily, as the name says, elders; deacons, as service people, are the most clearly defined, and perhaps deaconesses as well. But the organizational scheme in the various churches is vague, and even somewhat shifting.

IGNATIUS OF ANTIOCH (about 110 A.D.)

The room was scarcely large enough to contain nine men, and certainly it was not anything to boast about as a meeting place. It was barrel-vaulted, with one small, barred window high up; the walls were dirty and mildewed; the chairs were old and rickety; the table was somebody's long-ago discard. Nonetheless, it was called the "guest house" in the prison at Smyrna.

The elegant man who was obviously the host had arrived a week earlier in a coasting ship from Ephesus. He himself was from Antioch, in Syria, some two hundred miles farther south in the Asian mainland. He was under sentence of death. The condemnation had been affirmed by the court in Antioch under the new decrees of Trajan. He was not a common criminal, nor were the men with him criminals. Ignatius was the leader of the Christian church in Antioch, the center of Gentile Christianity in Asia Minor for the past thirty or forty years. He usually referred to it as "the church in Syria," although there were many other churches in the province.

The men had been talking earnestly for some time when there was a loud noise outside in the hall. A Roman soldier banged open the door and thrust in a slight young man. He half-stumbled into the room and the soldier bawled, "Join the rest of the pigs!"

"My dear Damas," said Ignatius, "it is so good to see you. You have come all the way from Magnesia, and I thank you. I am sorry that you have been treated so badly. You know these others, I am sure . . . Polycarp of Smyrna, Onesimus from Ephesus, and Burrus, his deacon. Here are Crocus and Epulus and Fronto, also from Ephesus. Polybius of Tralles is over there. And of course you know your own priests, Bassus and Apollonius, and your deacon, Zotion. It is so good to see all of you. Now that we are together at last, let us be together with the Lord Jesus Christ in prayer."

They began a song they all knew in praise of the Lord Jesus. Just then the door banged open again and the Roman soldier barged in once more.

"I told you to stop this racket or I'll throw you out," he warned.

He slammed the door and Ignatius got up despite his leg irons to see that it was securely closed. The next minute the door opened again, and this time the soldier appeared with a bucket of slops. He threw its contents over Ignatius and went off laughing derisively. Ignatius stood there wiping himself off as best he could while the others crowded around in dismay.

"Animals," Ignatius fumed.

"I wish I could do something," said Polycarp, who was the bishop of Smyrna. "If they were local police, I could use my influence here and get them to act halfway decent. But these legionnaires are beyond anyone's control."

"We must pray for them," said Ignatius. "I have ten of them in my detachment and they have been making this slow trip up the coast instead of sailing directly to Rome for the games, as they thought they were going to do. The more kindness I try to show them, the worse they act."

They stood ill at ease for a moment, as though an act in a play had come to an end and no one knew how long the intermission would last. Ignatius recovered first.

"I am forgetting my manners," he said. "Please sit down and let's try to forget it. I'm just an old condemned man anyway. But I am overjoyed that you have come from so many places so far away to console me. Tell us, Polybius, what is going on in Tralles?"

"Well," Polybius said, "I have good people. They truly love me, and they wanted me to come and tell you that they have the deepest respect and love for you too. However, I fear that they are being led astray, yet I don't want to scold them."

"What is the problem?" asked Onesimus.

"You have heard the same thing, I am sure, in your own places. We had a visitor last month who said that the stories we tell about the sufferings of Jesus Christ are just that—stories. No god could possibly suffer. He said that it just looked like Jesus suffered but that because he was a god, he simply brushed it all aside. No suffering, no pain, no blood. I didn't want to hurt anyone's feelings so I didn't say much about it, but it bothers me."

"Yes," said Damas, who was the bishop of Magnesia up in the Maeander valley. "We've had such people too. They just won't admit that Jesus was real. 'Make-believe,' they say. And that's the kind of religion they practice. They make believe that they are going to help the widows and the poor but they never get around to it. They talk about worship but they never show up when we celebrate the Lord's Supper."

"I've had them too," joined in Onesimus from Ephesus. "After all Paul said when he was lecturing in my city about the flesh and blood of Jesus, there are still some who can't admit that he was real. They have theories about everything but not much ever happens when they are around."

"And you, Polycarp?" asked Ignatius.

"Same here," replied the young man. "I thought we had trained our people well, but maybe all we did was to educate a lot of fools. I tried to lay down the law to them one day and they just walked out on me."

"Well, see here," Ignatius said, "we must do something about this. I think all of you know that if you love good disciples, you can expect no thanks. It's like those slaves who pine for release at the expense of the community and then turn out to be slaves to unruly appetites. I had some of those troublemakers in my own church. When I left Antioch, they were attacking the unity of the church. Thank God, I received a letter the other day telling me that peace has been restored, and I want to thank all of you who sent messengers to Antioch expressing your support. That did a great deal to bring people to their senses and to help them see the larger picture of what the catholic church is all about."

"I hesitate to be too strong about that, though," said Polybius. "I'm a lot younger than most of the very influential people in Tralles."

"Now," said Ignatius, "I'll repeat what I said to the people in Philadelphia, where some were disturbing the community, and myself too: 'Give heed to the bishop and to the presbytery and to the deacons.' Some, however, suspected I was saying this because I had previous knowledge of the division caused by certain factions; but he for whose sake I am in chains is my witness that I had not learned it from any human source. No, it was the Spirit, who kept preaching in these words: 'Apart from the bishop, do nothing; preserve your persons as shrines of God; cherish unity; shun divisions; do as Jesus Christ did, for he, too, did as the Father did.' When I sit in the midst of my corona with the presbytery and the deacons, I know that we must preach the truth we have received from the Lord Jesus and from the Apostles. The rank and file need us to safeguard the truth. We all have the same problems.

"Some want our people to go back to the old Jewish practices. That is bad enough, but not nearly as bad as these ancient fables that are utterly worthless, claiming that God cannot really come among us. As you pointed out, many of them say that his suffering was but a make-believe. Then why am I in chains? Why do I even pray that I may fight with wild beasts? In vain then do I die. My testimony is, after all, but a lie about the Lord. No, this is not a time to be hesitant. The bishop is to preside in the place of God, while the presbyters are to function as the council of the Apostles, and the deacons, who are most dear to me, are entrusted with the ministry of Jesus Christ. You must tell them that no one must undertake anything without the bishop and the presbyters; you must attempt to convince them that anything they do on their own account is not acceptable. Let the celebration of the Eucharist be considered valid that is held under the bishop or anyone to whom he has committed it."

"That's pretty strong," objected Polybius. "Are you sure this is what the teaching of John and Paul was?"

"We received, we give," answered Ignatius. "I know there are dissenters; there always will be. When I left Antioch, we had a dissension on our hands. But through your prayers and your show of unity, it has been healed. God is good who keeps us together in his church."

"Why did you send that delegation to Rome?" asked Onesimus.

"Well," said Ignatius, "now you have me on much less solid ground. I want and I don't want. They went for the glory of God. I wanted the Romans to hear from soneone else that I expect to die in Rome. I am not sure they would believe it from me. Onesimus, I want you to take a letter back with you and send it to Rome. You have better transportation than I and it will get there sooner. I suspect that some will try to use their influence to have me pardoned. You have heard that we have people close to the emperor in Rome; one of them is a cousin. They will think they are doing me a kindness, but I don't want a martyr's crown to slip out of my fingers."

"Aren't you afraid?" asked Zotion.

"Of course I'm afraid. I'm especially afraid that too much is being made of all this. Here I am on my way to Rome as a conquerer . . . forget those soldiers, they don't count. But everywhere I stop, I am hailed as a hero. Ephesus is a highway for martyrs. And I suspect that the Roman church will want to make a hero of me also. Am I dying for the name of Ignatius or for the name of Christ? And if for myself, will I run when the wild beasts are let out? Some people have. But I know what I want. I am God's wheat, and by the teeth of wild beasts I am to be ground that I may prove Christ's pure bread. Better still, coax the wild beasts to become my tomb and to leave no part of my person behind; once I have fallen asleep, I do not wish to be a burden to anyone. Then only shall I be a genuine disciple of Jesus Christ . . . then only, when the world will not see even my body. Those are brave words, and I don't know if I can believe them."

"Ignatius, Ignatius," said Polycarp, "you are caught between two worlds. And not the two you think. We have heard of how John longed to be a martyr but couldn't be. And Paul, who was. That's not unusual with us. But you are so sure of yourself when you are acting like a bishop and so fearful of yourself when you act as a man."

There was a long silence. Ignatius slowly rotated a bowl on the table. "A bowl is a bowl," he said. "Whether it can hold anything or not depends on which way it is turned. I know and I don't know. The church has been given to me by the will of God; my own fate seems too much in my own hands."

Bibliography

The letters of Ignatius are available in several translations. Notable is that of James Kleist in the *Ancient Christian Writers* series (Westminster, Md.: Newman, 1946). Besides the seven letters, we do not really have any reliable information about Ignatius. He dated his last letter August 24, but the year is uncertain except that it was during the reign of Trajan (97–117 A.D.). It seems an acceptable tradition that he was martyred in Rome. The best available study of the Apostolic Fathers in general seems to be that of Robert M. Grant, *The Apostolic Fathers,* Vol. I (New York: Nelson, 1964). There is also a good study of the Apostolic Fathers on the topic of priesthood by Manuel Miguens, *Church Ministries in New Testament Times* (Arlington, Va.: Christian Culture Press, 1976).

REFLECTIONS

The story told above is fictional in the sense that it describes a scene that we do not know actually occurred. The names and places and the concerns are known from the letters, however. The story form was used to draw attention to the personal aspects of the letters. The content of the talk and much of the very words are directly from the letters of Ignatius. Objections are sometimes made to the picture Ignatius draws of the bishop surrounded with his corona of presbyters and deacons, teaching and presiding at the liturgy. Theories have been advanced that the views of Ignatius were his alone, or that even his own church in Antioch did not go along with them, or that he at best represents a splinter group in early Catholicism, or that he was trying to manipulate the churches of Asia Minor and Rome into accepting his views. Such theories seem to me to be much more fictional than the story I have told here. The picture that emerges from the letters bridges the brief era from the apostolic age to the later developments that prevailed.

Even the style of Ignatius is paradoxical in the tradition of Paul. Ignatius is fond of balancing his sentences around the same verb used twice but presenting opposing senses. He is more intimate than Paul in some ways, but like Paul, he has a natural cadence of mind and an apt expression for antithesis. His letter to Polycarp is a curious mixture of a personal letter to the bishop and a community letter addressing the people. Logic and proof do not play a great part; traditions and images do. Nowhere does this appear more clearly than in the strong antithesis between Ignatius's assurance of truth when he is talking as a bishop in charge of a church and his personal ambitions and fears as a martyr-to-be.

Ignatius is almost presumptuous in taking for granted that all the churches would naturally honor him as a bishop and a potential martyr even though he was several hundred miles from his own province of Syria. He even seems to equate his own church of Antioch with "the church of Syria," although there were many other churches in that province, such as Laodicea, Chalcis and Beroea. He was the first to use the adjective "catholic" in speaking of the church, and he speaks of the church throughout the vast wide earth as though he knows that its unity is accepted. He has no doubts about his own dignity as bishop of Antioch in Syria. On the other hand, he is aware of his personal struggle to avoid bringing about his martyrdom just for the sake of his personal glorification. Yet, in another way, he desires this as the supreme achievement of his life. It is a curious interplay of certitude and doubt.

The primary objection raised to the Ignatian letters is that they say too much. There can be no doubt about their authenticity. There can be little doubt that technically there is a clear dependence on Paul, whom Ignatius sometimes loosely quotes from memory, or on John, whose Christological concepts he uses. There do seem to be legitimate connections with the organizational elements of the Pastoral Epistles. J.A.T. Robinson has theorized that the Pastorals are early, not late, dating them around 57–58 A.D. One may object to Robinson that it does not make much sense to have an organizational structure such as Ignatius depicts arise so early, especially when so completely void of intervening steps.

Other contemporary literature, such as the earlier letter of Clement of Rome and the later letter of Polycarp, seem to be basically in agreement with Ignatius; Hermas and the Didache are less so and place stronger emphasis on prophets. Which is the divergent model may be argued, but there does not seem to be any way of avoiding the fact that in these letters a regularized hierarchical structure is portrayed. The escape then must be into some of the other theories mentioned above. That there were various theologies in New Testament and apostolic times seems clear enough. That there may have been various models of organization is plausible. But that Ignatius was a total exception to the rule cannot be demonstrated from evidence. We simply do not have the facts to accept that.

Ignatius's understanding of the church centers around the consciousness that the glorified but still very earthly Christ is the center of everything. He is the invisible bishop. He has shared his authority with a limited number of others. As the Gospels take for granted that the Apostles were a special group, so Ignatius takes for granted that the corona of bishop, presbytery and deacons is distinct from the "rank and file," who harmonize as a choir with this special group. In every letter except that to the Romans, whom he had not met, he emphasizes the obligation of the people to be "submissive" or "obedient" to the bishop.

The clarity of this view should not be pushed beyond the evidence. The presbytery is patterned somehow on the old Jewish sanhedrin as counselors, and yet it has functions with the bishop of presiding at the Eucharist and at baptism; or it can even be commissioned by the bishop to perform these functions itself, much as the apostolic "band" in the Gospels. However, the precise functions of this group are not very clear in Ignatius, and it is always referred to as a group, with two exceptions for named people who are called presbyters. Deacons in some way are more clearly defined, and although they are always mentioned last, they seem to have far more importance than we give to such people in our present arrangement.

The Ignatian vision of bishops, priests and deacons becomes clouded in succeeding centuries. However, for the moment circa 110 A.D., when he wrote the letters, the concept of a separate clergy, with distinct responsibilities for teaching and presiding, was clear enough for practical application. Ignatius obviously does not claim such authority on his own personal merit or decision. When he confronts the issue in his personal life, he is much more hesitant.

AUGUSTINE OF HIPPO (354–430 A.D.)

The small, lively man in the black gown put down his quill and looked out over his little garden. The dry Saharan wind blew hot through the window, matching his mood of irritation.

"Hilarius," he called to his secretary, "what did I do with that tally?"

His secretary, a monk like himself, came shuffling over with papers in his hand.

"These?" he asked, knowing already what Augustine wanted. They had been talking about it most of the morning, sometimes in rough political ways and sometimes in more elevated conversation.

"Yes, yes," Augustine said as he took the sheets. "What were those exact numbers? Here!" He read the bottom line. "Two hundred eighty-six Catholics; two hundred eighty-four Donatists. What a lot of bishops for such a small country! If they had taken a vote, we might have lost. They certainly had more lay people than we did."

"They also had more 'good' bishops than we did," added Hilarius.

African politics in the fifth century A.D. did not involve only civil government, but religion and riots and military operations as well. Since the sack of Rome in 397 A.D., North Africa was the last prosperous province in the Empire, the breadbasket of the Mediterranean. But now prosperity was eb-

bing away, often abetted by the continual guerrilla warfare between the Roman landowners who controlled the port of Hippo
and the small farmers who raised the corn and olive oil on which
the economy depended. For the most part, the towns, especially
Hippo, were controlled by the Catholics and the rural areas by
the Donatists.

Augustine had once called Donatist assemblies a beehive
of clicking tongues—and worse. It was an odd and bitter quarrel.
The separation between Donatists and Catholics was not theologically profound, but it was deeply felt. In the persecution
of Decius, a lot of Catholics, including bishops and priests, had
compromised with the Roman officials and handed over sacred
books and vestments. "Traitors!" the sterner element cried.
When peace came, the loyalists would not accept the "traitors"
back. "No Catholic except a good Catholic," they said.

Moreover, the Donatists maintained that religious rites
performed by such men were worthless. So the obstinate and
bitter accusations began and continued for a half-century. First
the Donatist party seized church property and killed a number
of bishops and priests. Then the Catholic party retaliated and
there were martyrs on the other side. The group led by Bishop
Donatus (hence "Donatists") knew a good thing when it saw
one. Celebrating the deaths of martyrs was a great way to start
a protest demonstration. And celebrate they did, with banquets
and carousing and the beating-up of a few Catholics.

The Catholics had gained the upper hand both in the law
courts and in obtaining the support of the IX Legion. In 411
A.D., at a great meeting in Carthage, Augustine had humiliated
the Donatists. He had rammed through a proposal that Donatists, in order to retain their ownership of church property,
would have to come back into the Catholic Church by whole
communities. The government and the troops had backed him.

As Augustine looked out at his garden that morning, he
knew it had been a close thing. Getting Marcelinus, the Roman
governor, to validate the proposal was one thing; getting half
of the population to accept it was another. Even the humblest

politician could add the figures. Fortunately it was easier for the Catholic party to take back the dissidents than it would have been the other way around. If one wanted to join the Donatist church, he needed to be rebaptized; if a priest or deacon wanted to join, he had to be reordained. On the other hand, Augustine had grown realistic enough to know that if he could count only "good" Catholics as his followers, he was a minority leader. He needed all who were baptized, whether they did anything about it or not.

Augustine had deeper convictions than that, but he was an experienced street-fighter, perhaps even a bit dirty. If all Donatists claimed to be "saints," obviously the least scandal among them was grist for the mill. Augustine collected all the scandalous stories he could find and published them in pamphlets that were distributed freely. The Donatist martyr feasts were particularly offensive to him. He denounced the wild goings-on in churches, the drunkenness and the shouting. Thank heavens, his house was in a part of town where he did not have to listen to it.

There was, of course, more substance to his opposition than that. All morning he and Hilarius had been discussing just how far Augustine ought to go. He had begun in a much milder tone twenty years earlier, when he was still a priest and spokesman for Bishop Valerius in Carthage. He had written to a friendly Donatist bishop, Maximinus:

> I was even seeking an occasion for a talk with you, so as to smooth out, if possible, the small remaining difference of opinion between us, when lo and behold, a few days ago, the news reached me that you had rebaptized our deacon Mutugenna. I felt very deeply both his wretched lapse and, my brother, your unexpected backsliding. I know, indeed, what the Catholic Church is. The nations are the inheritance of Christ, and the ends of the earth are His possession. . . . To rebaptize a heretic, who has received this sign of salvation, according to the Christian custom, is certainly a sin, but to rebaptize a Catholic is a monstrous crime.[4]

Augustine was by natural bent an elitist and a scholar. He delighted in good conversation, philosophical discourse and the best reading. He read everything he could lay his hands on and seems to have written down every thought he had. Such a man had to think of himself as being different from others. He was one of the best known men of his day, and he had gone through a colorful conversion crisis. Then he had written a book about it. It was natural enough for him in the days of his early fervor to think that everybody in the Catholic Church ought to be at least somewhat like himself: wholehearted and dedicated. But experience as a bishop had shown him that the real church was something different. To make his point, he often used the story of the net let into the sea. The net contains good and bad fish, all swimming around together. But it does not belong to us in this age to sit on the shore and sort out the good and the bad fish. We simply tend the net, no matter how bad it smells.

Augustine's theological conviction was better than his political acumen. As he grew older, he became more tolerant in his acceptance of human fallibility. The church was for the world; the church could be the world. If people got no farther than baptism, well then, one had to accept them. And if the ministers who did the baptizing were no better than the people, well then, one had to accept that also. But Augustine always hoped for more.

He had gathered a group of like-minded men around himself in Hippo. They lived as monks in a monastery while they took care of the somewhat curious business that Augustine generated. Most of Augustine's day was spent as a Roman patron settling disputes among his retainers, Catholic or not. He was a political power in town, and he had connections across the sea. He was Hippo's most famous citizen, and he used his influence to the hilt. But he kept in mind that his power was to be used for all, not just for the good.

On the other hand, he also thought that power was to be

used decisively. Africans seemed obsessed with the idea of God the Judge, Augustine promoted that thinking. His most frequent admonition referred to how God would judge. And he had a Roman legion to back him up. Late in life he regretted that he had relied so heavily on brute force. But then, he took a very serious view of those who drifted off.

Like many another Roman, he instinctively thought in military terms. Baptism and priestly ordination, he said, were like the tattoos branded on the backs of the hands of soldiers in the Imperial armies. They made the identification of deserters easy. Christ the Emperor was entitled to recall to his army those who had received his brand. The "brand" was called a "character," and so the idea of permanence passed from Augustine into the vocabulary and thought of the Christian church.

Although the question of priestly character was not at the heart of the dispute, it was bound up with it, as well as with much more important ideas. Augustine knew that the Roman world was on the way out. He tried to preserve for the future as much as he could of Roman order and honesty. It was essential for him that the old republican virtues be incorporated into the church and that the church survive for the good of all. Honesty in commitments, whether as a baptized person or as a deacon or a priest, was vital. A commitment was not just a personal experience that might sustain one in an exemplary life for a while. It was a mark, a dedication, a meeting of words and actions in ritual that truly accomplished an inner change.

Augustine lost. He won the battle against the Donatists but lost the war in North Africa. He died in his study in 424 A.D., while Hippo was under siege by the Vandals. They conquered and wiped out all the warring Catholics and Donatists.

Bibliography

The best biography of Augustine seems to be Peter Brown, *Augustine of Hippo* (Berkeley: University of California Press,

1967). His letters in the "Fathers of the Church" series, Catholic University, are very interesting.

REFLECTIONS

In the long run, Augustine was the most important Roman leader for centuries in saving what could be saved of the old order. The stabilizing force of authority in society was soon to pass from the Empire to the church, and that church was served by a corps of permanent ministers. Celibacy came to be the widespread rule in the next centuries and the priestly leadership had to become self-perpetuating by reason of excellence, not by family inheritance. It was for better and for worse, but "character," although we do not read of its being discussed much in the next centuries, was a central factor in the survival of Western civilization and the church.

The incipient church order that had slowly emerged out of the New Testament movement and coalesced rapidly in the second century A.D. had become the Establishment by the time of Augustine. The orders of society were in place: the bishops, who seem to have been numerous and very local; the priests, who were the caretakers; and the deacons, who seem to have been the cutting edge in society. The concept of "sacrament" emerged as something the Holy Spirit imparted, especially in baptism, and it could not be lost. There were problems with how to deal with the recalcitrant, and measures tended to become increasingly harsh as time went on. "Public penance" became the social weapon that kept people in line. The clergy were in danger of being cast in the role of policemen. But they were much more. They were the custodians of law, of culture and of whatever order could be salvaged from the barbarian invasions. They also became the amalgamators who evangelized the barbarians. They were the one stable corps of social agents in a dissolving world.

3. The Era of the Fathers

Most surprising is the quick emergence by 100–150 A.D. of what was later called the "monarchical episcopacy."[5] How Clement of Rome, Ignatius of Antioch, Irenaeus and Polycarp came to be leaders and by what means they were given their office is unknown. We do know that each of them exercised a teaching office; it is principally from their writings that we know them, and that is sometimes about all that we do know of them. In this office they sometimes appear together with a "presbyterate." They claimed to preserve the authentic Gospel against opposition while explaining it more fully for special communities. In addition, some of them appeared at times with the council of presbyters as the liturgical officers. This triple leadership of bishop-presbyter-deacon is revealed clearly in the Ignatian writing; in Rome and some of the Pauline churches, other terms and other schemata are hinted at but not as clearly stated. However, it was the Ignatian model that became the tradition. "Presbyter" begins to be translated into "priest" in the second century, although there was a great shifting back and forth in the use of the terms priest and bishop (especially with the later introduction of "chorbishops," i.e., rural bishops) until the fifth century.

By the late second and early third centuries, the ancient liturgies (particularly the Liturgy of Hippolytus) began to describe the ritual for the designation of these men. Much was said of choice ("election") by the community, but there was always an imposition of hands and a prayer that the Holy Spirit may send upon them a gift. Obviously the community did not think it was merely installing its nominees. The real ability to act as priest was seen as coming from the Holy Spirit. The sacramentaries clearly state that these chosen people were set aside from others, "elevated." There are fairly clear implications in the texts that this was seen as part of a divine arrangement.[6]

The actual organization into bishops who presided and priests who assisted was slower in developing; the data is meager. Apparently, in the original setting of small and scattered churches, the bishop and his council of priests presided immediately at the Lord's Supper and other ceremonies such as the baptism of catechumens. Still, the priests were considered a college of presbyters and must have had some counseling role in the teaching office, but we do not know in what way. As the number of the baptized multiplied and spread into the countryside, the need for local leaders made itself felt and the priests acquired increased authority and autonomy. The distinction between "clerics" and "laity" had already existed for a long time, going back, perhaps, to Clement of Rome before 100 A.D.[7] By the fourth century, the distinction was clearly operating to provide for the needs on both sides. No priest could be ordained without a congregation. Thus the Council of Chalcedon in 451 A.D. decreed that no one should be ordained as an "absolute" priest, i.e., one who was not attached to a local church. The intimate relationship between the priest and the community was extremely important from a practical viewpoint at that time; the prohibition was later changed when times changed. Perhaps it is this rapid development of the bishop-priest-deacon system that accounts for the large number of "bishops" in North Africa during Augustine's time.

All of this developed while the notion of the nature and extent of the church was still emerging. Indeed, it developed while the nature and very existence of Roman society was being challenged. In the often acrimonious disputes over doctrine in the first five centuries, opponents were quick to "excommunicate" one another. It was Augustine's vision of the City of God and the City of Man that finally put limits to this factionalism and focused on common ground. The key points were the realization that baptism, once accepted, could not be lost; that the church was catholic in the good it could bring to the whole world, and holy even when it was not visibly so in its individual members. With typical Roman sense, Augustine insisted that those branded with the sign of the Emperor Jesus could always be brought back. With this went the similar view of priests and deacons as those signed with a *sphargis,* or "character," that could not be lost. It was not a peripheral idea tossed off by Augustine in the heat of argument, *pace* Kung,[8] but absolutely central to the practical alignment of the church as the preservator of society in the Dark Ages, which reasonable men already feared. Although character was not a topic of speculation in the next eight centuries, it certainly was the undergirding for the preservation of order in the church, applicable to both laity and clergy. During those same centuries, celibacy was promoted not so much as an elitist and ascetic practice derived from monks, but as a discipline for the core cadre of diocesan leaders. It was the surest sign of what the church stood for in an increasingly ungodly and uncivilized world.

THOMAS AQUINAS (1225–1274 A.D.)

The banquet was proceeding smoothly even if in a somewhat dull fashion. The friar had been broodingly silent. Suddenly he shattered the decorum of the king's table by bringing down a meaty fist that made the dishes rattle and saying very firmly, "That will settle the Manichees." Of course nobody had been talking about Manichees. He called his secretary and said, "Reginald, write this down." The king, who was sitting next to him, waved Reginald away and called a secretary of his own. He knew that what was to be said was important.

The extraordinary scene took place around 1269. The king was Louis IX of France; the friar was Thomas d'Aquino, and the setting was Paris. Thomas did not ordinarily take his dinner with kings; this was a command performance. But the two men had much in common. Later on each was canonized by the Catholic Church as a saint, which was more surprising in the case of Louis than that of Thomas. More to the point, however, each was a shrewd political realist.

Thomas was no stranger to politics. His father was the "count" of Aquino, bearer of a rather insignificant title to a small area between Rome and Naples. Italian politics was made up of such small fiefdoms, and this one was just on the border between the Kingdom of Sicily, ruled by Frederick II, and the papal states. The Aquinos were Frederick's subjects, but they were also loyal supporters of the Pope. That made matters difficult when the Pope excommunicated Frederick in 1269. One of Thomas's brothers, Rinaldo, had been executed by Frederick in 1243 for going over to the Pope. His brother-in-law was killed in battle. The family castle at Roccasecca was attacked. Thomas was no longer at home when all this happened, but he was always close to his family. He visited them whenever he could, and indeed, in his last illness it seems to have been his sister, Teodora, who noted his serious change of character. Suffice it to say that he had seen soldiers mustered and defenses amassed; he had lived through times of uncertainty when rumors of war and hordes of marching armies were rife; he had been involved in enough family and papal politics to know the shifting sands and the treacherous undercurrents of power. He knew what power was all about, and he had seen it exercised rather bluntly.

At one point in his life, Aquinas even wrote a treatise on politics. Nobody paid any attention to it, but it seemed to him to be important, and especially important because it dealt with a contemporary situation. University professors held public debates on the issues of the day and circulated their views in writing. Thomas was no egghead. He did an incredible amount of writing, which today may seem to us overly abstract. His best-known work, the *Summa Theologica*, actually was written to give young students a solid textbook.

So Thomas was not interested in Manichees as a scholarly footnote to something (he never used footnotes himself). What was important was up front. Manichees were important to both Thomas and Louis as a contemporary problem; both men shared the view that beliefs and convictions were extremely pragmatic and extremely dangerous. Both of them got into fights and neither walked away from them. Both of them were interested in what happened to people in the face of conflicting ideas and looming battles. Thomas increasingly came to think of himself as having a special apostolate to young students for the purpose of guiding them in the way of reasonable truth. Faith was all right, but it had to be reasonable. Louis was also a defender of basic virtues, and sometimes of traditional ideas. But he was one of the most reasonable monarchs France ever had; the concepts of reasonable law and justice for all were fundamental to his thought.

In fact, it was an emerging society that these men were trying to guide. The old feudalism, with its attempt to establish a place for everybody and to secure stability, had never quite worked. It had been overly dependent on the taboos and half-superstitious customs that a closed society breeds. While the new universities were beginning to discover a brave new world, they were uncertain about leaving the old and familiar one.

One of the challenges to the Establishment came from the new mendicant Orders of Franciscans and Dominicans. An unforeseen emergence of brilliant professors among these unattached friars had provoked a conflict at the University of Paris, the acknowledged intellectual center of Europe. The universities were really run by a Corporation of Masters, who were most jealous of their privileges and their seniority. For years on end, the masters had confined themselves to electing secular priests. On merit alone, some of these new friars had to be given place. The masters did not like it. They saw the friars as agents of Rome who were going to try to whip them into shape. There was enough truth in their apprehension to make it a talking point. Moreover, who wanted to invite into this elitist group these new friars, who seemed to have no need and no taste for the privileges of the Corporation? Besides, how could a wandering mendicant be a proper scholar? The masters even questioned his capacity to be a proper priest. So jealousy as well as shrewdness coincided when a new star arose in the person of Thomas d'Aquino, an Italian Dominican, who had received his license to teach as a master from this very University of Paris.

They made him wait. It took a papal bull and a direct order to the chancellor to induce the Corporation to suspend its rules about minimal age and give Thomas an appointment.

Then Thomas turned about and joined the radical opposition—very politely, of course. To bring more reason into faith, he began to use the recently translated works of Aristotle. It was the claim of Aristotle that life was reasonable and that men fared best when they saw the order in all things, physical, social and spiritual. Thomas's opponents claimed that the faith of Christianity could not be confined to reason, and some of them— Bonaventure and Scotus in particular—were very reasonable and saintly men who simply looked at matters quite differently. Thomas was willing to admit that the foundations of faith are revealed and beyond reason; but once known, he claimed, they can be reasonably accepted and fitted into a pattern able to govern human life.

Thomas actually wrote little about the subject of priestly ordination. In his earliest teaching, which dealt with the traditional commentary on the "Sentences of Peter Lombard," he described the Sacrament of Orders as a power that was granted within the person of the priest, enabling him to function within the church. Thomas was rather worried about such a power attributable only to priests and thereby tending to cut into the freedom of all Christians. Nonetheless, his somewhat revolutionary hypothesis seemed to him to be the basis of everything else about Order.

The key word was not "priest" or "sacrament," but "Order,"

for so this office within the church was traditionally described. It did establish an order within society. That, of course, was to the advantage of Thomas and the mendicant friars. It was a development from Augustine's concept of character. It did not hurt in the argument with the seculars of the Corporation of Masters that Rome was all for order, which it controlled.

Years later, at the end of his life when he was lecturing in Naples, Thomas returned to the question of the priestly Order. We do not have his direct words; this section of his *Summa Theologica* was written by someone else from sources we cannot quite identify, but it undoubtedly reflects some of his concerns at the time. The *Summa* is similar to his earlier treatment, but in it he returns twice to the question that had bothered him before, namely, that of priestly power trespassing on the freedom of the baptized. The Supplement to the *Summa* does, to some extent, concentrate on the cultic functions of the priest, including several concerns that seem unimportant to us, such as the institution of vestments. By that time, Thomas had come to the conclusion, as evidenced elsewhere, that the church had the ultimate spiritual power, but he was not prepared to go beyond that. He seems to have become increasingly disillusioned about the other kinds of power churchmen exercised. By and large, Thomas's final view reflected an ordered church establishment that functioned well within medieval society.

Bibliography

The most convenient biography of Thomas is by Angelus Walz, *Saint Thomas Aquinas* (Westminster, Md.: Newman, 1951), commissioned by the Master General of the Dominicans. Cf. also Thomas Gilby, *The Political Thought of Thomas Aquinas* (Chicago: University of Chicago Press, 1958).

REFLECTIONS

Thomas did not add greatly to the concept of priesthood. He gave a reasonable explanation to views already accepted. He thereby clarified previous notions and left to his generation and succeeding generations a set of formulae that could be readily understood and built upon.

Basically, Thomas said that the old Augustinian concept of "character" was to be explained as a "power" (in Latin, a *potentia*, an important technical word). This power was somehow ingrained in a man and made him capable of performing acts that others could not perform. It was not a commission by the church, which would have been simply something external, nor was it simply a "call." It was not a license to minister (the medieval universities knew much about "licenses"), nor was it a personal act of commitment. It was an "obediential potency" modifying the soul of the priest, thereby conforming him to the person of Christ in certain actions.

For Thomas, these actions centered around the Eucharist. All that a priest did was geared to promoting cult, either directly or indirectly. That was part of his personal life. As Thomas grew older, he seems to have become more aware that he was not a scholar for the sake of scholarship, but a priest who was called to the apostolate of educating young men in theology. Liturgy meant much to him. Traditionally he is associated with the cult of the Eucharist in the liturgy of the feast of Corpus Christi. He was a frequent preacher; he spent much time as a "lector" instructing young Dominicans, who were a clerical society. Although little is said of a sacramental ministry, he did see his activity as priestly.

However, in his reasonable explanation of the "power," he wanted it to be known that he considered this power as purely spiritual. Whatever other power had come to the church in his society, he did not link it with the priestly power. As a matter of fact, he seemed increasingly to be uncomfortable with that idea.

Beyond his reasonableness, Thomas was something of a mystic. Undoubtedly his early biographers exaggerated the unusual and sensational in his life. After all, apart from his writing, he did not seem to live a very exciting life. One of the more authentic stories is of his final days. On November 6, 1273, he had some sort of psychological and spiritual experience in Naples. He suddenly turned to his companion, Brother Reginald, and said, "I can't write any more." And he did not. Shortly afterward he was visiting his sister, Teodora, and she asked of his Dominican companions, "What is wrong with Brother Thomas? He is not himself." Five years of intense study and writing had left him completely exhausted, if not more. The attempt to be reasonable about all things had taken its toll. He remarked, "Everything that I have written seems to me to be so much straw." The Christian world has judged otherwise about the writings of this great theologian. But Thomas himself was aware of extensions beyond his reasonable world that could not be put into words.

He died a priest. He had resisted all attempts to deflect him from his Dominican vocation. Neither the usual joys of family life nor the blandishments of becoming an archbishop or a cardinal could draw him away from his free choice of being a friar. And that was his choice. Priesthood was something else.

What Thomas did for his time was to stabilize the concept of priesthood on spiritual powers. Popes of the period were as much military and political leaders as they were priests. Bishops were lords; priests were concerned about becoming abbots and having assured revenues. Thomas pointed out that the essence was the service of the Eucharist. But he still insisted that this was a "power," dangerous as the concept might be.

Medieval Christianity preferred Thomas's earlier picture of priesthood. It worked. Priests had power in many ways, and they continued to use it until the Protestant Reformation forced a change. Many of the Reformers just abolished the concept of priest and substituted that of "minister." The medieval need for order, in which everyone knew his or her place, simply could not be stretched to accommodate the expanding world. In a way, Thomas was responsible for that expanding universe. The Renaissance and the industrial revolution would not have been possible without the emphasis on rational cause and effect. It led to ways of living that Thomas did not anticipate.

4. The Medieval Order

As the centuries rolled along, the church acquired many old Roman (and sometimes Byzantine) ways of conducting business. The clergy were the principal agents of such social transactions. When the Augustinian theses of sacrament and character again began to be discussed in the medieval universities, it was again with an emphasis on order. Obviously the discussion was about matters society thought important. Order was exercised both by the church administration and by the civil government. The distinction between the two was often as obscure as the conflicts between them.

Popes were not only "servants of the servants of God," but kings and military adventurers as well, along with a great number of other things having little to do with being servant to anybody. It was not unusual for the local bishop to be prince as well as shepherd. Just where the authority once claimed for preserving the purity of the Gospel stopped and the authority for ruling in this world began was very unclear. It was during these times that the "two-sword" theory of ruling developed, but the two swords were more often clashed than pointed in the same direction. Aquinas brought a reasonable explanation to the nature of the Sacrament of Order and of the character that was involved; he stood for the "power" of the sacrament, but he was not able to resolve the question of where the authority began and where it ended. Obviously he thought it a very important question.

CHARLES BORROMEO (1538–1584)

In Milan on October 26, 1569, the archbishop's chapel was crowded for evening prayers. A few feet behind the archbishop a man was elbowing space for himself. He drew a huge revolver and aimed at the cardinal's back. The gun exploded with a roar. The room filled with smoke; people screamed; the assassin began to flee. Charles Cardinal Borromeo fell to his knees, knocked down by the impact. He stayed there a short while and then he slowly rose and motioned for the Vespers to continue as before. Later they found that although the ball had hit his spine, in some way it had not even broken the skin. When the Milanese heard about it, they shouted "Miraculo!" and began to recount other wonderful stories about this man: how a rainbow had appeared on the night he was born and how the delegate of his enemies had died on the way to Rome. It was a very strange ending to a very hot political fight that Charles seemed to have been losing.

The cards were always stacked against Borromeo as a reformer, as if to test how far he would go. He was born into a noble family in northern Italy; his mother was a Medici and his uncle on her side was Pope Pius IV. He should have been a perfect example of all the corruption that was so much denounced by the Reformers of the 1500s. At twelve he was given title to an abbacy that carried no spiritual responsibility, only the right to a substantial annual revenue. At twenty-one he was appointed archbishop of Milan, although he was not even a cleric and was not sure that he wanted to be one. A year later he was a cardinal and at twenty-one, the secretary of state to his uncle. He was the principal spokesman and manager for the Pope at the decisive third session of the Council of Trent in 1542–43, but he had a speech impediment and could scarcely be heard.

After the Council, Borromeo finally prevailed upon his uncle, the Pope, to let him visit Milan. He had been ordained priest and consecrated bishop by that time. There had been no resident bishop in Milan for eighty years. He settled down in the city and began to live in a simple style, which shocked the Milanese. This archbishop was on the job and meant business about reform.

Among the traditional privileges of the archbishop of Milan was the right to have an armed guard with some police powers. Borromeo revived the custom and used that legal precedent to arrest one of the most scandalous nobles in the city. The Spanish governor, the Duke of Albuquerque, objected but did not take decisive action, although the Senate of Milan denounced Charles Borromeo. Then Charles claimed the right to set things in order at the rich church of Santa Maria della Scala. When he tried to enter the church, an armed scuffle took place and the processional cross was shot from his hands. Borromeo excommunicated the whole college of canons at the church. Then he moved in on a particularly rich and corrupt little group of lay monks called the Umiliati. That was too much; they hired an assassin, one of their number by the name of Farina. The Umiliati were confident that popular opinion was behind them since by that time Charles was in hot water with the Duke of Albuquerque, King Philip II his sovereign, the Senate of Milan and his own diocesan officials, and possibly the Pope. He was more of a Reformer than they had bargained for. However, Farina was a singularly inept trigger man and must have loaded his gun improperly. That was not the way the Milanese interpreted it. With their cry of "Miraculo!" Charles became a hero overnight and "our cardinal."

Charles wanted first to reform the bishops and priests of his archdiocese. He told them at the beginning that if they were to give marching orders to their people, they had to be at the head of the column. He himself gave an example of simple and austere living. Then he set the pace for hard work in keeping up with the business that priests should do. He held regular synods to organize the archdiocese. He set about educating future priests to meet his standards. Some of those who were priests could not even read and write Latin; some did not know the simple rites of administering the sacraments; many of them were living high on the hog from the accumulated wealth of previous centuries, and a good number had mistresses. Charles established a seminary, staffed by Jesuits, for his future priests. The students in those first years numbered about one hundred forty, but that was enough to turn the tide. Later he established another seminary for students who were of solid piety but not intellectually up to the standards the Jesuits demanded.

He was a tough-minded and efficient administrator. He knew exactly what he wanted to do and he insisted that it be done in precisely his way. In compensation, he delivered results. Everything he did was well-planned and exactly executed. There were those famous little black notebooks, some of which still exist. In them he jotted down in a minute scrawl such divergent items as the tools and seeds that Alpine farmers told him they needed and the fact that Father Francisco Bossi kept puppies with elegant collars in his bedroom. These things were never forgotten. Action followed.

Charles worked harder than anyone else. He was one of those men almost impervious to heat and cold, rain and sleet, tastes and smells. On his tours of the Swiss Alpine areas of his archdiocese, he could outclimb most of his staff, biting in with ice ax and spiked shoes; he could arrive at a remote, crude village and sit with the "sheep who stank like goats" and discuss the people's problems in their own patois. When the plague hit Milan in the summer of 1576 and lasted for the next year and a half, it was Charles who roamed the streets organizing relief and shaming the civil and ecclesiastical leaders to come back. On one occasion he heard a baby crying in a plague-ridden house that nobody would enter. He fetched a ladder, climbed in the window and rescued the child. He could also be surprisingly mild and forgiving when he had made his point.

Charles Borromeo died in 1584 at the age of forty-six. He was "our cardinal" for the Milanese, and undoubtedly he and the men he trained saved northern Italy for the Roman Catholic Church. He was an extremist in some ways, but then he was an extremist with himself. He prayed: "God save Charles or Charles will destroy himself."

Bibliography
There is a surprisingly good biography of Borromeo in *Butler's Lives of the Saints* by Herbert Thurston and Donald Attwater (New York: Kennedy, 1956), Vol IV, 255–262. Cf. also the delightful portrait by E. H. Thompson and Margaret Yeo, *The Prince of Pastors* (New York: Longmans, Green, 1938).

REFLECTIONS

The Reformation was not ultimately caused by an abstract conflict over whether one is saved by faith or by works. The Roman Church knew well enough that it was endangered by a lack of works. The system had grown rotten with worldliness on the part of the clerical management. The most important decision of the Council of Trent was to reinstitute seminaries. Not much was said about priestly ordination. The ancient formula was repeated that the sacrament imparted a character and that priests could not go back to being laymen and that ordination could not be repeated.

The statement was hardly necessitated by a movement to reordain priests in the dissident churches. Quite the contrary. The problem was a rather embarrassing one for the Council Fathers: They could not stop priests from leaving the Roman Church. Yet indirectly they had to say that even extreme worldliness or the most unworthy of motives could not absolve one from the obligation to lead a soundly spiritual life. Priestly ministry did not belong to a man because he was good or because he was selected by others to perform certain functions, as some of the Reformers said. It was conferred and that was that. The only way back was by personal reformation of life.

Charles Borromeo was a catalyst in putting the Council of Trent into action. He was hated by many. A number of European governments would not even allow the decrees of the Council to be published. Too much real estate and political clout was at stake when the church tried to change the status quo. The whole power structure was against it.

It took a man like Borromeo to provide the kind of leadership the common people would accept and that forced change from below. He managed to combine two things the people needed: He got results, and he gave them a sense of dignity beyond their humdrum lives. Charles always believed in magnificence when it came to church affairs. He poured on all the brilliance of liturgy; he encouraged Palestrina and other musicians, and he hired the best architects to redecorate the churches. He gave people visible evidence of what their money was doing for them. And then he gave them a sense of mystery. They acclaimed him as "miraculous" because they needed miracles in their lives. And he went far beyond ordinary human endurance in the kind of virtue he exemplified. He made the humbler virtues seem possible because of his own extremism.

He clearly saw that if change were to be permanent, there had to be a stable agency of change. In the last days of his life, half-dead, he insisted on journeying to Ascona to inaugurate his new seminary for Swiss priests. He believed in the system, and he backed it with prudent and vigorous action.

5. Reformation and Reform

The Reformation offered a radical religious and social solution to many festering problems of the period. The corruptions in ruling authority were numerous and deep-rooted. Some of the early Reformers simply abolished all notion of priesthood and sacrifice. The primary agent of religion became a minister who had only one basic function: to preach. For that he or she needed only community delegation. The importance of liturgical officiating was later brought back into many of the churches of the Reformation, and even the word "ordination" was used, although the old concept of character never did quite reappear.

The reform of the Roman Catholic Church began with no great development of speculative explanations but with much of practical definition. The Council of Trent in 1563 defined Order as a sacrament and numbered it among the seven sacraments (a great amount of discussion had previously ensued over the number of sacraments). It also declared that Order conferred a character, that those ordained did not revert to the status of laymen if they did not preach, and that Order could not be repeated. The Council did not define the nature of this character, and obviously nobody was enthusiastically promoting the repetition of ordination, as the Donatists once had. Quite the contrary. Unless the defining of the existence of character by Trent is to be taken as a total irrelevancy, it must be seen as important in reestablishing a new order. The Reformers were principally interested in abolishing the old ideas of character and elitism in order to change the nature of the church; the unreformed within the Roman Church were looking for an easy way out of permanent obligations and spiritual responsibilities but they did not want to change any of the temporal order. So the tenor of the Council's decision—which, along with its legislation about seminaries, is often considered its most important work—was to reaffirm the unique and unchangeable nature of the priestly status.

The centuries following Trent were centered on an attempt to implement its rulings. Charles Borromeo, and later the French school, succeeded in establishing seminaries and bringing about a reform in the priesthood. The French school was most important in centering the whole dignity and dynamic of being a priest on imitation of Christ the Priest. All lesser motivations were kept firmly secluded. Vincent de Paul worked imaginatively and untiringly to provide practical images and living examples to the priest of Jesus Christ. The university-based education of the Medieval Ages was replaced by a distinctive and somewhat isolated clerical education. Holiness and service, not scholarship, were the key elements. It was this ideal of the priesthood and this method of training that passed to the United States, especially in the seminaries conducted by the Sulpicians and the Vincentians, which is to say, most of the early seminaries for diocesan priests.

THREE
Contemporary
Problems

1. A Survey of Official Statements

Vatican II abolished many familiar images in the church. Sometimes it replaced them, sometimes it did not, or the new ones did not click. It should not be surprising that the crisis in priesthood is often expressed in a conflict of images. Conflict has been more normal than unusual in priesthood history, as we have seen.

The depth and the extent of the changes introduced by Vatican II are subject to varied interpretation. For some, they are essential structural changes in which the laity has been put on a par with the hierarchical organization and assigned almost identical functions. The only problem now is to make these changes work efficiently.[1] For others, the change has been more cosmetic than real. As the functions of the priesthood have varied widely over the course of history while the basic ingredient of the ministerial priesthood has remained the same, so now the functions of the laity have changed without making any

real change. From this viewpoint, the main problem is to preserve enough of the older images to retain the heart of the
"traditional" ecclesiology. Probably resolution is some mixture
of the two; at least both elements are under discussion, sometimes with a violence of words.

The Council itself wrote a document on "The Ministry and
Life of Priests," which did not substantially modify the existing
images. It cited the usual theological explanations of the nature
of priesthood. It dealt with the usual functions of priests as
liturgical ministers and "rulers" of God's people. It spoke of
the priest's relations to his bishop, to fellow priests and to the
laity. Then followed a long section on the spirituality of priests,
much in the stream of the French school of spirituality, with
exhortations to all the usual pious practices. Two of the few
new things introduced were a brief reference to the presbyterate, which was stressed even more in the "Decree on the Pastoral
Office of Bishops," and a reminder that priests had a place in
the world.

In other documents the Council sometimes veered away
from the conventional *in persona Christi* interpretation by dropping reference to the power of the priest and speaking of the
ministry of the church. The problem with all of this was that it
fitted rather awkwardly with the new images of the People of
God, which had been created in the "Dogmatic Constitution
on the Church." On the other side, it came into conflict some
years later with papal instructions that priests were not to be
candidates for elected public office, especially highlighted with
the photograph of Pope John Paul shaking his finger at Fr.
Ernesto Cardenal.

The Roman Synod of 1971 dealt with problems in the
priesthood and began rather well. "Does the priestly ministry
have any specific nature? Is this ministry necessary? Is it true
that the priesthood, of its very nature, cannot be lost? What
does being a priest today mean? Would not Christian communities be sufficiently served by presidents designated for the
preservation of the common good, without sacramental ordi-

nation, and exercising their office for a fixed period? Is the present-day church too far removed from its origins to be able to proclaim the ancient Gospel to modern man in a credible way? Is it still possible to reach the reality of Christ after so many critical investigations? Are the essential structures of the early church well enough known to us that they can be considered an invariable plan for every age, including our own?"[2] To say that the questions were better than the answers is probably to forewarn ourselves that our own answers will be insufficient.

The "Code of Canon Law" of 1983 also attempted a new vision of the pastoral function and the authority of bishops, priests and deacons. These "sacred ministers" were ordained for the sake of the church both as the People of God and as a society. Toward the People of God, the Code stressed among other things the responsibilities of the ministers to provide sacramental care, preach, know their people, help the sick, instruct, provide examples of Christian living and to be witnesses to Gospel values. Within the society, they were accountable to authority, responsible for serving the community for which they were ordained, forbidden to take an active role in politics or trade unions, to name a few of the parameters.

The Code also tried to take into account the legitimate rights of the "laity" to be heard and to exercise the apostolate in the church. The problems here are that the law does not change much even though its expression may be modified. The working principle of "ordinary power" was retained. Ordinary power is that which adheres in an office such as bishop or pastor, and it needs no delegation from above. No limits were set by the Code on this "ordinary power," either in teaching or in administering. Of course, merely publishing the law in 1983 in no way assures that actions and attitudes will conform to it.

The Canon Law Society of America protested the lack of any due-process procedure for the settlement of grievances.[3] The Code, in its preparatory stages, was criticized for clericalism. Thomas J. Green protested somewhat strongly: "This principle of fundamental Christian equality does not permit structures reflecting a stratified ecclesiology, dividing the People of God into two classes. It requires the complementing of a vertical authority structure with a horizontal structure of solidarity. Such a principle does not admit of paternalistic patterns of governance inadequately sensitive to the profound spirit of community that should characterize intraecclesial relationships."[4]

In 1967, the National Conference of Catholic Bishops authorized a full-scale study of the priesthood in the United States. The study was to cover data in eight separate fields. Five of these areas were reported on in 1971, namely scripture studies, systematic theology, historical investigation, psychological study and sociological investigation (the so-called NORC study). The report on systematic theology was not accepted. Then, in 1972, a permanent committee was established that subsequently published reports on priestly spirituality, authority, priestly growth, priestly ministry, and research and scholarship. A summary report, which had involved substantial financial grants and the involvement of many persons, was made in 1974.[5]

Unfortunately, this process, which sounds rather well-organized, had been derailed for a while by the Subcommittee on Systematic Theology. This lengthy study by nine prominent theologians was scholarly and primarily conventional, although it reflected current theological approaches.[6] On several points it seemed to downplay "tradition," whether theological or disciplinary is not clear, concerning character, women's ordination and celibacy. In these cases, the emphasis was apparently on present need as understood by the writers rather than on tradition as a guiding principle.

By way of contrast, the Sacred Congregation for the Doctrine of the Faith issued its declaration on women's ordination in 1976. Its core statement was: "The Church's tradition in the matter has thus been so firm in the course of the centuries that the Magisterium has not felt the need to intervene in order to formulate a principle which was not attacked, or to defend a law which was not challenged. But each time that this tradition had the occasion to manifest itself, it witnessed to the Church's desire to conform to the model left to her by the Lord."[7]

Whatever may be said of the Congregation's conclusion as such, it is quite obvious that the subcommittee and the Sacred Congregation were operating from quite different models of what should determine the nature of the church. In 1977, USCC issued a new study entitled "As One Who Serves," carrying greater pastoral orientation and avoiding these delicate questions.[8] It did adopt from the previous Subcommittee on Systematic Theology the image of the priest as "servant-leader," a title that seems to have gained popularity from a treatise on management.[9]

2. Research Projects

The results of a number of research projects on priests and seminarians in the United States have been published in the past twenty years (notably the NORC study[10]), chiefly through the initiative and financing of the bishops themselves. They indicate a primary problem concerning authority structures. The problem is not whether there should be such structures, nor whether bishops should be strong leaders. This is admitted by the great majority of priests. The question is how the authority should be exercised and to what extent. For example, there is no doubt about the ancient right of the bishop to call his church back to the authentic interpretation of the Gospel. Whether that right extends also to telling priests which insurance company they should deal with is a different matter. This is a caricature, to be sure, but it illustrates a weakness in the principle that, by itself, is indefinitely applicable. There is also the question of how the bishop should dialogue with his presbyterate, a question that affects the relations of priests with their communities as well.

Both bishops and pastors have "ordinary" power, as the new Code continues to assert. Most priests sense the problem in practical affairs, and that worries those among them who are canon lawyers. The Code does not define the parameters of that authority, whether it is limited to doctrinal matters, disciplinary matters, administrative matters or others. It is simply left unrestricted. So too is the bishop's power. In times past, bishops and pastors have sometimes taken to themselves power to make all decisions within their field of operation, no matter how remotely connected with church business. The problem seems insoluble. It was this very question that bothered Thomas Aquinas, and he seems to have despaired of resolving it: How is priestly power compatible with the freedom of all the baptized? Previous efforts to define the precise limits of such power have generally proven futile in the church's history except for hearings or investigations in specific cases, and then the decisions have not always been accepted. As a result, today the church in the United States is uneasy from top to bottom over an uncertainty that many people seem unable to handle.

3. Theological Discussion

Note was made in the last chapter of the immense amount of recent theological writing about the ministry and priesthood. For our purposes, we need to reexamine the basic conflicts involved. They seem to revolve around two foci: the equality of all the baptized in the responsibility for ministry; and the nature of sacramental character, with all of its consequences.

Those who differ with the customary premises also tend to read differing practical conclusions. These usually center about: 1) temporary priestly service, 2) the abolition of mandatory celibacy, and 3) the ordination of women. Perhaps there is also a jurisdictional dispute involved between the control that Rome apparently wants to keep over priests and the autonomy of local church communities, but it has not captured the popular imagination as clearly as these others. Let me attempt to give as honest a recognition to all viewpoints as I can, although that is probably a vain hope since one side is in possession and there are strong feelings on both sides.

As has been said often enough, the problem of priesthood depends largely on one's view of what the church is and how it came to be what it is today. It should be noted that this view is ultimately a matter of an act of faith. Unfortunately, no historical study, however detailed and accurate, can prove by iron-clad developmental steps that the church today in all its aspects is exactly as its Founder intended it to be.

When Jesus ascended into heaven, the shape of the church was clear in some respects and quite fuzzy in others. The same is true of other theological problems such as Christology. The earliest writings (Paul's, for example) have a good deal to say about who Jesus really was and his ongoing effect on the conduct of human affairs. But the development of those truths required a number of centuries and some very difficult controversies. So also with ecclesiology. After Christ's ascension, the church began to function as a somewhat amorphous body, first developing in local areas with varied leadership. Early in the next century, clear patterns of local leadership emerged. Then the churches became aware of cohesion within various areas, probably more so as local persecutions or heresies affected them and drew them together for support. When the church became the public religion under Constantine, a further coalescing of worldwide (i.e., Roman worldwide) catholicity made itself felt. By the fifth century, the unity under the Roman pontiff was effective and capped the organization of Pope, patriarchs, bishops, priests, deacons and laity.

One can no more prove the historical inevitability or the logic of this expansion than one can prove that Christ himself wanted the successor of Peter to live in Rome. All one can do is to point out the data indicating the various trajectories, some of which survived and some of which fell by the wayside. No immediate argument can be made that since something was done or not done in the earliest times, or in some one segment of development, it is normative practice. Obviously, the development over twenty centuries has not been totally consistent; like the biblical history that preceded it, it is full of starts and stops, developments and recessions, new interpretations and reinstatements of old ones. The interpretations proposed today are often echoes of the past as well as new sounds in our world. How they should be judged is not entirely clear. Nor can an apodictic argument be made that if the church did something for the wrong reasons, such as limiting priesthood to males only, it must stop doing it. The church is the depository of the essential faith, not of logic. Much of its decision-making has evolved around a question of human prudence and may well be questioned. The extent to which we are free to change in a new prudential decision is also unclear to us at times.

Those who begin with the equality of all the baptized as the ones sent to evangelize the world—Edward Schillebeeckx is probably the foremost exemplar—point to the New Testament indications of charisms of service that were given indiscriminately.[11] A favorite text for illustrating this is: "There does not exist among you Jew or Greek, slave or freeman, male or female. All are one in Christ Jesus" (Galatians 3:28). The text occurs in a passage in which Paul is speaking about the relation of faith and law, not about Christians as ministers. It is misappropriated here, but it does summarize the spirit of the approach. From the New Testament the trajectory leads in this argument to the early Christian literature, in which the community as a whole is described as the bearer of the authentic faith and the bringer of the Good News to all. When the bishop-presbyter-deacon triad begins to emerge, this approach highlights the role of the community in electing, or acclaiming, the one to receive the leadership of the community.

The conventional picture, especially as found in Roman documents, is quite different. It begins with the Apostles and their powers, connects with the episcopacy as reflected in Ignatius and the later Roman Fathers, picks up some emphasis from the French school of spirituality (which stresses the identity of the priest with Jesus, the High Priest) and ends with a picture of the priest as a distinctive officer within the church. The early separation of clerics and laics is taken for granted, and the role of the laity in this picture is much downplayed.

Vatican II, in its "Constitution on the Church," did bring back into some prominence the role of all the baptized, and the "Declaration on the Life and Ministry of the Priest" does mention the priest as the witness of the faith of the community. But it is fairly clear in these statements that a Scholastic notion of *in persona Christi*, as meaning that the priest in some way does represent Christ in his mediatorial role, is being reflected.

That is admittedly the point of the dispute, and it is brought out by the tendency of both sides to champion one view to the detriment of the other, to exaggerate the incompatibility of the two approaches, or even to reach conclusions that seem divergent from the facts or methodology used.[12] On more sober thought, both sides would admit that the community of faith is the mediatorial agent. Both would admit that charisms are distinct from office and that office attaches necessarily to some in the church for the sake of leadership in the faith. Yet the distinction is not clear, and inevitably confusion and conflict ensue.[13]

Perhaps an example, not too farfetched, may illustrate. Let us say that a married couple has been appointed to minister to a small parish that otherwise would not have a priest. Let us say further that they are professionals, with Master of Divinity degrees, and that they were hired after consultation with the local parish council. They live in the parish rectory, visit the sick, organize study groups, encourage social concerns, instruct children and converts, preside at para-liturgical services when the priest cannot be present, bury the dead, and perform other functions of this nature. All of this is quite legal and contemporary. Now the question arises as to how they are different from the priest, who may be their inferior in education as well as in pastoral skill. They cannot preside at the Eucharist or administer the Sacrament of Reconciliation, for example. Why not? If they have been doing their job well, they probably represent the faith of the community better than the priest, who only occasionally appears. If the community were to delegate them as its leaders, what would be lacking except the prayer of a bishop? And why could that not be had if all the baptized are equal? Or is there something inherent to the priest by the call of the church through the bishop and the calling down of the Holy Spirit in prayer and the imposition of hands, all of which separates him from others, even those who may have more appealing charisms?

The second main point of disagreement is "character." Does character make an insurmountable difference? Let us begin with the more conventional view as illustrated in Jean Grelot and most of the Roman documents.[14] The explanation derived from Scholasticism says that character is an ontological fact, that is, it changes the nature of the Christian in some way so that he becomes capable through an "obediential potency" of performing actions in the name of the church that others, lacking that particular charism or gift, cannot do. In a popular way, we used to speak of putting priests on a pedestal, not simply for personal holiness (which could well be doubted), but because of position, which was theirs alone.

On the other hand, Bernard Cooke and Thomas O'Meara, in excellent treatises (note that Schillebeeckx seems to avoid the question), have proposed a newer way of looking at character.[15] They observe that the problem of defining "character" comes down to making a distinction and then a connection between charism and office. Charism is a gift for service given by the Holy Spirit without regard for the official status of the recipient. That is a simple fact of observation. For example, some Christians are good at patching up quarrels, some are good at teaching their religion, some are good at consoling and some at counseling. Charism has nothing to do with one's status in the church, whether as lay person or cleric, to use the ancient terms.

Priests are chosen because they have at least some recognizable gifts of leadership that the community needs. Like any other Christians, they may have other gifts and these may be immensely diverse. However, these men are set aside by the community in a unique ritual that has, as far back as we can trace it, involved the laying on of hands by someone admittedly superior and an invocation of the Holy Spirit that a special grace or power may come upon them for the good of the community. This is office.

In this view, character is not an ontological power, but a new "relatedness" to a function that is to be performed within a community and toward a community goal. It is not the same as the common priestly character of all the baptized.

> Each Christian, by virtue of belonging to this community, participates in this responsibility and is obviously therefore empowered to profess his faith sacramentally in Christian liturgy. The priestly character in which one shares does not point to one specific function in Christian life. Rather, it is a fundamental, all-embracing specification of one's human existing; it conditions one's entire life of faith and grace by placing it in the context of priestly purpose. This is not an individual modification that comes to each person with baptism; it is the Christian community that is priestly/sacramental in its whole being. . . . It is different when one speaks of a sacramental character resulting from ministerial ordination. Here, it is a matter of specific directedness to some function that enables the community to express its priestly character.[16]

The above explanation by Cooke certainly directs attention to the connection between the common priesthood of the baptized and the ministerial priesthood. It certainly directs attention away from a quasi-deification of the person of the priest. But on the other hand, it does not answer clearly the question of what constitutes this "directedness." Nor is it clear in what way this is compatible, if such is intended, with the older notions expressed by "character."

Another historical factor may be added: These persons designated by the Holy Spirit form a "college," or "presbyterate," that assists the bishop in his role of witnessing and preserving the authentic faith of the community. Even though "office" may itself be a charism, it is a distinctive kind of charism, tied in with a permanent community need that touches the very preservation of the community of faith as such.

The newer view of character is apt to emphasize, however, the character of this gifted person as acting in the name of the community. This character is permanent in the Christian faith community, and its public recognition in one person is unrepeatable. Thus Trent's declaration on the existence of character is explained.

All of this frames an interesting speculative argument which is certainly legitimate. However, it is the resulting effects on the image of priests which is really the point of dispute. In reality, the speculation itself could lead to the same pragmatic accommodations from either side of the argument. The older Thomistic view could be accommodated to a temporarily exercised priesthood, married clergy and perhaps also ordination of women. It does not ordinarily do so for reasons which are not within the speculative arguments themselves. A mildly changed image of priests might result from the arguments of the newer theology. Ordinarily, it does not.

One should recognize at this point that personal involvement begins to influence the conclusions. We all have a natural tendency to vindicate our present status in society. There is also a natural tendency for opposing parties to draw the wagons together in a circle when under attack and to want to appear as liberal or as conservative as their neighbors. One should not presume that all of this is pure academic research. The images begin to have dominating power.

The conventional image about permanence in the priesthood is too well known to need repeating. "You are a priest forever according to the order of Melkisidek," and there is no way out of it, although one may be suspended from public exercise of the office either through the imposition of a penalty or the granting of a dispensation. But priest one remains. The conventional picture of character then begins to assume concrete form. A priest is not a priest because of personal holiness, although that is expected both theologically and publicly. Even faith is not the determinant as long as he is joined to the church sufficiently to want to do what the church does in these priestly actions. The priest is set aside from others by something within himself. From this it is deduced that his spirituality should be different from others; his life-style is expected to be different; celibacy is fitting, even though all admit that it is not a divine requirement, but a disciplinary practice.

The contrasting view is that there is nothing really different about a priest except that he does different things, such as preside at the Eucharist. Function rather than essence is said to distinguish him. But the functions are service actions, and those who receive them have a right to receive them as efficiently as possible. Consequently, the priest is first of all a professional minister for the good of others. His qualifications, his life-style and his job performance should meet professional standards.[17] Thus it is sometimes proposed that priests be selected from among those most professionally qualified, that they serve temporarily, either as they wish or as the community wishes, and that they then have the option of returning honorably to the lay state. Celibacy has no great significance in this pattern, and indeed, it may be counterproductive. It is at best a personal choice.

The ordination of women often appeals to similar understandings. The emphasis begins with the equality of all the baptized and then goes on to the concept of professionalism as the determining criterion. Women are as good as men both theologically and professionally. Add to this a realization that the condition of women is changing in our society and a presumption that the original dispensation of male only ordination was made on the basis of social prejudices and the conclusion for women's ordination is reached. Whether a different pattern of clerical status is desired than the present male priests have devised is sometimes not clear.

Behind the ideological differences about theology, a real power struggle is quite obvious. Who's the boss is still the bottom line.

As noted in the Declaration on Women's Ordination, the basic premise of the official position is simply tradition. Tradition is the necessary criterion of church teaching. Male ordination is clearly one of the oldest and most universal practices in the Catholic Church. If this is a truly theological tradition, then considerations such as the changing social needs or attitudes, the historical situations in which male only ordination began, or whatever success or failure the male priesthood may have had are beside the point. If we are dealing with a universal practice instead of a theological tradition—and that point may be argued—then the advocates of women's ordination are simply facing a very strong disciplinary tradition which is in possession. However, it should not be assumed that the male only proponents are simply afraid or prejudiced. Their solution to fostering the dignity and equality of women in the apostolate is through administrative reorganization, a good deal of which is already in place. This certainly does not solve the problem of the power struggle, but does put it in a more appropriate context. The basic question is not one of rights, but of willing service to others.

TIM DEMPSEY, THE IRISH PRIEST

The Monday-morning edition of the *St. Louis Post-Dispatch* carried the news item: "RIVAL GANG CHIEFS AT DEMPSEY INVESTITURE. 'JELLY ROLL' HOGAN AND 'DINTY' COLBECK SEE 'FATHER TIM' ASSUME RANK OF MONSIGNOR." It was understandable that the Fourth Estate was more interested in the gang warfare in St. Louis than in ecclesiastical dignitaries. And that was a mistake.

It all began when Willie Egan was gunned down in October, 1921. The warfare was over the booze business during Prohibition, and a mean little war it was. Father Tim Dempsey gave Willie the last sacraments. Then he began a quiet round of private talks with over thirty of the rival gang members in an attempt to keep violence off the streets. His efforts succeeded sporadically, but after a running battle between two carloads of gangsters on Locust Street that sent Abe Goldfeder and Max Gordon to the hospital, hopes for peace collapsed. It took Father Tim until April of the following year to persuade Ed Hogan and Dinty Colbeck to sign a truce. The public announcement of the pact was their attendance at Father Tim's installation as a monsignor on May 10, 1923. Even the newspapers thought it was fitting.

Father Tim Dempsey was the picture of the Irish priest. He was six feet two, over two hundred twenty-five pounds, and in the usual phrase, he had the "map of Ireland written on his face." He was known to have used his fists to floor particularly rowdy customers; he was made an honorary member of the Teamsters Union for having settled difficult strikes. His parish in the slums of St. Louis was not all that Irish anymore. By 1898 when he became pastor, most of the Irish had made it and moved out. They were succeeded by the Italians, the Russians and the Polish. Then there was the floating population of unattached men who had not yet made it anywhere: transients, unemployed and desperate. Drunks, hoboes, prostitutes and petty gangsters drifted through the streets on the near north side. Naturally, Father Tim took them all in. He never lost his brogue and he never met a person who was not Irish. He once commented about his gangland friends: "The poor misguided b'ys that do be killing each other, and the fathers of them the decentest men that ever came to America."

He provided beds for the outcasts, both men and women. He started a nursery, and of course he had a soup kitchen. During the depth of the Depression in the 1930s, he housed over ten thousand a year and fed thirteen thousand a day. He mediated almost fifty labor strikes on the simple proposition that it would not do to let families sit at home without food. He settled the Public Workers' Association strike in 1936 on the assurance to the men that he would get them a fair deal. Two thousand of them returned to work the next day on his word.

Father Tim had no time for books or plans. He never read a book on economics in his life. During the Depression, he was asked by a newspaper reporter about his plans for feeding the hungry during the coming winter. He replied, "Son, I never made a plan in my life. All I'm going to do is, by the grace of God, to keep right on feeding those who come day by day." He thought that social workers who investigated the "deserving poor" were simply wasting time.

I have a boyhood recollection of Father Tim. One Sunday morning my father took me to St. Patrick's. I remember watching the crowd flow out into Sixth Street after Mass. A few cars were trying to move and a streetcar was making slow headway. On the sidewalk across from the church a group of men were shooting dice. A little farther on a huge truck with a suspicious-looking cargo was trying to back into an absurdly small door in a warehouse. On that side of the street a shiny Cadillac was parked, presided over by two men in somber suits. And in the streetcar tracks, amidst all the crowd and noise, Father Tim was walking up and down, reading his breviary. It fit.

Father Tim died in 1935 of a heart attack. He had finished a busy weekend of work and set out to visit his sister on Sunday afternoon, but first he stopped at the cathedral to go to confession. (It was an odd act for a man who in public life was the very epitome of optimism and confidence.) He died the next day while relaxing at his sister's house. He was sixty-eight years old. He had been a young priest of twenty-eight when he had arrived as pastor. He told the archbishop at that time, "If Your Grace will only send me to St. Pat's, I give you my word I'll never leave the parish till I die." He kept his word.

He enjoyed the vigorous life that burst around him. Like

many high achievers, he simply found life too good. Someone asked him if the many distressing stories he heard did not dampen his spirits. He said no, that it gave him joy to know that he was able to relieve the distress of the people through the kindness and generosity of those who placed the money and supplies in his hands. He was no reformer of "systemic evil"; he simply took care of one job after another. And he had a ready laugh for the problems. His brother was a police sergeant who at one time asked him to help apprehend one of the transients at Father Tim's Hotel for stealing an overcoat. Father Tim wanted to know whose coat had been stolen. His brother replied, "The archbishop's." Tim smiled. "Who could better afford to lose an overcoat?"

Father Tim is buried among his poor in St. Louis. He bought a plot of ground to provide a last resting place for them and named it "Exile's Rest." He never let them forget that there is more to life than simply the scrambling for the next meal. They did not call him Father Tim for nothing.

Bibliography

Harold McAuliffe wrote a biography entitled *Father Tim*. Tim Dempsey is also noted in John Rothensteiner, *History of the Archdiocese of St. Louis* (St. Louis: Blackwell-Wielenday, 1928). The background data is largely from H. Paul Douglass, *The St. Louis Church Survey* (New York: Geo. Doran, 1924).

REFLECTIONS

Tim Dempsey was the real-life movie version of the ethnic priest. He fit the part. It did not matter that he was Irish and that his friends were Italian and Russian and Polish. The American church was the escalator for the unamalgamated and the upwardly mobile. They were transients, no matter whether they were drifters or later immigrants soon to follow the Irish into the suburbs and the better jobs. Tim Dempsey and his like helped them. They needed a leader; especially they needed someone who embodied for them the possibility of providing aid in their upward swing. It might be only a decent bed for the night; it might be only someone who treated them with dignity. But it was a step up.

The syndrome affected the church structure itself. Those were the years between 1900 and 1950, when the clerical ranks swelled. The priesthood itself was an escalator. If the parish priest did sometimes put on airs, he was accepted as having the right to do so since that was what they all hoped to achieve. The church was a promise of better times and the priests were the visible assurance. They were not out of sight; they were part of their people, very much so. And they were the part that all hoped to become.

Amidst the grime of the slums, the church was the haven of beauty. The churches built in those days testified to the magnificence of the vision of common people that beauty belonged among them. No one today would presume to build a church on the scale that was then automatically taken for granted. St. Pat's in St. Louis was not a "magnificent pile," as the stereotyped expression went. But in the depths of the Depression, Father Tim planned to beautify it. He died before he got around to it, but the trade unions did it for him after his death. The church and its priests offered something of the mysterious beyond to people who had so very little, and it was not simply "pie in the sky." It could be seen.

The American church succeeded because it brought together groups that were apparently disparate to begin with and made of them a real community. Neighborhoods mattered; church societies mattered; sacrifice and responsibility for the church mattered. There was pride and defiance, and sometimes violence, in their midst. But there was also assurance.

Father Tim's vow that he would stay at St. Pat's until he died meant that he saw many others move on, and he bade them a congratulatory good-bye. He was ever the center of the community's life. His people needed him. And he needed them. He would be an anachronism today, despite the similar needs that still exist among many. The cohesion is no longer present. The Catholic Church in the United States changed not so much because of Vatican II, but because the ethnic patterns of community stopped operating after World War II.

A great deal of credit belongs to the unusual outpouring of women into the teaching communities of the American church in those days. Year after year they educated the young, insisting on standards of excellence that made the escalator work. They were also an inspiration. Together with the priests, they created hope and belief in a better future. But they never let anyone forget that there was a greater hope than that of simply getting ahead. The vision of the priests and sisters was nobler than that. If they were at times somewhat rigid and narrow in their discipline, they at least taught that there was something worth accepting discipline for. The center of life was the church, and the center of the church was the Eucharistic presence, which was so often celebrated magnificently. A quiet place of prayer among stained-glass windows and the muted glow of flickering sanctuary lamps were greater symbols of what it was all about than a shiny new car for Father.

The image of the priest was that of a man of action: He worked for the people. But the image was not simply achievement-bound. The priest was not esteemed only because he had made it and they had not yet done so. When the reaction came later, we parodied the tendency to "put the priest on a pedestal." There was a temptation, especially among the Irish and the Germans, to make him so holy by ordination that he did not represent the constituency. Perhaps the ideals, both worldly and spiritual, were too high. But at least the essence of the priesthood was not ignored.

4. The American Situation

The conflicts that emerge here are not uniquely Catholic problems. The role of the churches in the public life of the United States has shifted rapidly, especially since World War II. First, it should be noted that according to a Gallup poll in 1976, the American Catholic Church was no longer thought of as an ethnic, immigrant church.[18] Until the end of World War II, white Anglo-Saxon Protestantism had been the dominant coloration of American public life. Catholics had been, and had thought of themselves as being, a tolerated minority. The Irish, Germans, Italians and Central Europeans had brought their cultures with them, most of which revolved around the church. They were "foreigners." They wanted to become accepted Americans, and the price was often the surrender of the customs and ways of thinking that united them as a social group. The American public in turn had to surrender in great part its antagonisms; being defensive was no longer a priority issue with Catholics. For example, after World War II, Catholics no longer had to fight the Ku Klux Klan; the American public was on their side. The election of John F. Kennedy is usually pinpointed as the decisive date.

Second, the whole social Gospel changed for all religious groups after World War II. What had been a dominant theme in evangelical Protestantism for fifty years no longer appealed to the public. Catholics had been involved in social problems for a long time, especially during the Depression, when there was a virtual working coalition between labor unions and Catholics. "Catholic" and "Democrat" were almost synonymous in social concerns during the New Deal, and there were many priests involved in the labor movement, often on the front line. Catholic action was never quite "catholic" in the sense envisioned by the Papal Encyclicals and the hierarchy, but at least it was "action."

Then Catholics discovered after World War II that they could not precisely define their social program. Moreover, the labor unions faltered in their bid to stand as the dominant social influence in the country.[19] As Catholics were increasingly assimilated into the total culture, they became like other Americans in their attitudes toward anti-war and anti-race issues. In the old ethnic scene, priests were concerned with the poor, the

out-of-work and the racially deprived, but their concern was on
the basis of "my parishioners." As student protests and racial
riots demanded the attention of all citizens, there was no dis-
tinctively Catholic stand. Bishops, through the National Catholic Conference of Bishops, have long taken positions on larger
issues of public policy, notably on nuclear war and economics
in recent years, but they have been well ahead of their constit-
uencies.

Third, we have now reached the stage where a power struggle for the control of "civil religion" is taking place.[20] Along
with Catholics, the evangelical and the mainline Protestant sects
seem to form an indistinct coalition against fundamentalist sects
and a growing secularization of the culture. Catholics themselves
(and in their own way, the other sects also) are divided. The
divisions between progressives and traditionalists that have
emerged among Catholics since Vatican II have not been clarified; the growing divergence between Roman ways and an inherent democratization in the American church seems to be
persistent and sometimes unnegotiable. We keep repeating the
platitude that "the church is not a democracy," but we do not
really know very clearly what it is. Vatican II stressed "community" as the base unit, and we have not yet figured out how
to deal with that. We cannot organize our muscle to exercise a
dominant voice in the public life of the republic.

These are issues that affect priests deeply, whether they
are aware of them or not. The place of the priest in public
debate is uncertain. What is the priest's area of life and what is
the laity's? Or is that a false division? The laity seem to have
moved quickly into the priest's previous area of ministry, but
the priest seems to have been excluded from what was formerly
the laity's space. Ten years ago the younger clergy were in favor
of abandoning clerical clothing and all the paraphernalia of "the
clerical ghetto." It does not seem to have paid for many admission tickets and they are moving back. This is noticeable
in the research on seminarians, which indicates a growing tendency on their part to become more clerical.[21] Students are no

longer greatly interested in social concerns; they *are* greatly interested in spirituality. That this is simply a temporary fad, evidence of a new vision of priesthood, or simply narcissism, is not clear. The age of liberalism seems to be on the wane in many areas of concern. We seem to be in a second wave of change after Vatican II.

Vatican II was not responsible for all the changes in the Catholic Church, perhaps not even for most of them. Vatican II did at times reflect a concern for community over and above hierarchy. Infallibility was the prerogative of the community before it was the responsibility of those in charge.[22] Ministry to the world was the responsibility of all the baptized, not simply of the clergy. Diversity, not uniformity, became the desired matrix of growth.

During the sixties and early seventies, these programs of Vatican II were reflected in the seminary education given prospective priests. The "in word" was to join the *mainstream* of American life, not to be separated from it by a distinctive education. We joined professional accrediting associations. The culture "outside" was in shock and conflict. Blue jeans and Brooks Brothers suits, Woodstock and Madison Avenue, protest marches and barricaded university presidents, hippies and yuppies and a thousand other pictures jostled one another. The same turbulence was reflected in its own way within the seminaries. Conflict and change were often the ruling enthusiasms. It was within this context that the changes in the church (and churches) began around 1965.

Elsewhere in these pages I have tried to caricature the priest in *Going My Way*. It is odd that the image is so well remembered after so many years. Whether through nostalgia or rejection, the picture still evokes a response. We yearn for a simple solution. No other image has entirely replaced it. And so we have a fundamentalist reaction today, and it shows up in unusual places. We now have permanent deacons; they are often more pontifical than the run-of-the-mill priest. That is a superficial observation, but it does seem at times that we are in danger of becoming another "mystery religion" by denigrating what the mystery really is.

Finally, add to this that nowadays the structure of the American Catholic Church has become largely that of the American corporation. One need only look at all those Catholic centers and their burgeoning directorates. Staff meetings, reports, the flow of paper and the levels of decision-making, the pecking order, who gets how much money and so forth—all these follow the practices of American business, including management seminars, counseling services and retirement benefits. Bureaucracy has taken over, and with its usual inevitability, it has produced work situations in which the final result is sometimes busyness instead of apostolic zeal.[23] In practice, one often wonders if anyone is listening. Responsibility to one's office, not to the next higher committee, seems to be vanishing. Decisions sometimes seem to be made more autocratically than previously.[24]

The argument here is not that this is wrong. Obviously American business management has a great deal to commend it and the church should (and probably inevitably will) use it. The problem is to recognize the innate tendency of bureaucracy to war against our spiritual convictions. The ancient legal tradition of ordinary power, however many problems it may have, is a needed corrective against this. In the final stage of a bureaucratic system nobody really has ordinary power.

FATHER TOM, THE STATISTIC

Mary Hurley sat darning socks. There really was no reason for her to be darning socks at this time except that she always did it in the evenings, just as her husband Jim went bowling on Tuesday and Thursday evenings. It preserved her sense of order.

She looked up from her work at her husband, who was reading the evening paper.

"What's eating Tom?" she asked.

"Hmm . . . what's that?" said Jim as he tried to fit her words into his cogitations over the sad status of the Cubs.

"Something is wrong with Father Tom," she said. She was referring to their oldest son, associate pastor at St. Gilda's, ordained fifteen years ago and golden boy of the local clergy, apparently.

"Oh, that," said Jim calmly. "That pastor of his giving him a hard time again?" He was referring to Monsignor Lavery, known to be a sometimes benign and sometimes catty despot.

"That's just it," Mary said. "It's not His Exaltedness anymore. This is something I can't understand. Tom used to gripe about us in the same way he did about the monsignor, so there's nothing new in that. But now he's talking about liberation and subsidiarity and irrelevance and things like that."

"What are all those things about?" Jim asked. "I never could understand priest talk. Seems to me if they just kept on the ball and did their work the way the rest of us have to, they wouldn't have time for all those fancy ideas."

"Well, maybe so," said Mary. "And I sure can't understand him. When he used to come home, he would sit around in the kitchen and talk and I could at least understand what he was talking about. But now he seems to be using all this fine language because he can't talk about what he really wants to say. He's almost getting to be a stranger."

She sat quietly and mulled it over for a while. "Do you think he's going to leave?" she finally asked.

"God knows what for," Jim said as he turned a page. "I suppose he has some lady friend among those fine people out in Hawthorne, but he ought to have enough sense to know that he's not that great a find. Fine boy he is, even if he is beginning to forget a lot of what we taught him."

"He always seemed so enthusiastic when he was going to

the seminary," Mary said as she put down her darning. "Come to think of it, we didn't see nearly as much of him in those days as we do now. And yet he always seemed so much closer to us. He has changed."

"Well," said Jim, "it's his life and he'll figure it out for himself. We all have our problems. I've got the Cubs and he's got the monsignor."

Meanwhile, the subject of this conversation was having dinner with Ed Michalski at the local athletic club. He was halfway through the soup and halfway through his own tale of dissatisfaction. Talking with Ed seemed the only safe lifeline to what had been. Neither of them were dressed in clericals, but most of the club members knew who they were anyway.

"No, it's not Lavery," he was saying. "The old boy isn't that bad. At least he keeps me in pocket money. This is on him tonight. No, that's not it. The old thrill just isn't there anymore."

He put down his soup spoon and stared off into space as though he could see old Tim Flavin, his spiritual director in the seminary, chomping on a cigar and saying, "Don't create too many heavens, kid; they ain't out there."

"I used to think I was doing something important when I went on communion calls," he said. "Now I don't know. All I'm doing is providing some old lady with a break in her dull routine. I could do as much if I were delivering the paper or reading the meter. And those mechanical confessions; I used to laugh occasionally. I don't anymore."

"What's wrong with you?" Ed asked. "Bad case of Vaticanitis? You've been reading too many books."

"Maybe," said Tom. "There just doesn't seem to be anything that we can do. All those good things said about how the church was changing, but just try something new and see how fast you get slapped down. The last people with any clout in this church are the guys like you and me, who do the work. Get a plush chancery job and you have some push."

"Why don't you depose the archbishop?" suggested Ed.

"Power to the people. Who needs a bishop anyway? Hire some-body to do the confirming and ordaining and we'll get a manager for the diocese."

Tom laughed. "The odd thing about it," he said, "is that I think the archbishop should be more of a leader than he is. All those toothless declarations about being in favor of good as long as it doesn't hurt anybody and against evil if somebody else is doing it—they just don't seem to cut the ice. For God's sake, why can't he occasionally brush somebody back from the plate with a high fast one? We need leadership in this diocese."

"Leadership but not discipline?" Ed queried.

"That's not what I mean and you know it," said Tom.

"Not quite, old boy," answered Ed. He settled back for some serious talk. "How do we get all these fine conclusions of leadership without some way of putting them into effect? You're on the Priests' Senate. Why don't you do something about it?"

"Priests' Senate, my eye," Tom said indignantly. "We're not even a rubber stamp. A debating society at most. We talk and talk and then we send up recommendations to His Excel-lency and nobody ever knows if they have even dented his skull."

"Why, I heard him complain the other day that his hands are virtually tied since the Senate started operating . . . has to consult everybody before he can do anything."

"And that's another thing," Tom said. "Since we started all this consulting, I've been talking to fewer and fewer people. Even old Lavery is having a staff meeting every Monday morning now. We talk about everything that everybody is going to do, but it just gets more complex and less real. Sometimes I yearn for the old days when Lavery would bawl me out and I would curse back at him. We seemed to have more to say then that was worth saying."

"How's Carol?" asked Ed suddenly.

"Oh, she's all right. She probably feels as bad as I do. Now her community wants her to get a degree in social service because they're pulling out of the schools. Something about serving the poor. I think it's a crocked pot, but she seems to feel that it's the center of the world. I just don't know."

"Why don't you pull out?" suggested the devil's advocate. "Be a hero. Show them there's a better way."

"I can't."

"Why can't you? It's done every day. There were Charlie and Gus, even old Hopmeier. If you don't like it, stop being miserable."

"No." Tom was silent for a while. "Do you remember Ed Flynn?" he finally asked.

"Of course. First man out. We all knew Ed was going to leave. The faculty didn't have any doubts. We used to kid him about giving him a layette for his ordination present. Whatever happened to the bimbo?"

"Something happened to me there. Like you say, everyone knew that Ed was fooling around. We probably didn't take it as seriously as we should have. But one little thing stands out in my mind. We were all talking about it and we were all on that preordination cloud nine. About a week before ordination I was roaming around one night when I saw lights on in the chapel. I stopped by to see what was going on. No one was there except Ed Flynn. He was all dressed up in full vestments and standing at the main altar practicing Mass. I couldn't figure it out. It would have been odd to see anybody doing that, but Ed Flynn? It just floored me. I don't know what happened. I dropped down on my knees and cried."

There was a silence. Ed Michalski had enough sense not to say anything.

"Look, Ed," Tom went on after a while, "I'm not John of the Cross and I don't have visions, but there are some things that hit me and stay with me. I knew what was going on in Ed Flynn's mind, the push and pull in two directions at the same time. I knew it was going on in my mind too. We all played those games of 'what if . . . ?' But I couldn't stand seeing what it was doing to him. It wasn't honest and it stuck out like a whore in a meeting of bishops. You just don't do that kind of thing. When I was ordained, I took seriously what was happening. When the bishop put his hands on our heads and we realized what they told us—that the Holy Spirit was coming down—I really did feel something. It's not all bilge water, you know. It's real. That's why I can't leave. I'm lonely and I'm tired of fighting city hall. But I can't leave."

REFLECTIONS

Father Tom, the Statistic, is a fictional character, which is not to say that "any resemblance to living persons is purely coincidental." The story is modeled on the NORC survey of 1972 (*The Catholic Priest in the United States: Sociological Investigations*: ed., A. Greeley, Washington, D.C., United States Catholic Conference, 1972). This survey, commissioned and paid for by the bishops, sampled over six thousand priests, active and "resigned," on over six hundred items. It was very thorough and has, unfortunately, been too often ignored.

The data was collected in 1969–70; in other words, shortly after Vatican II, when both enthusiasm and dismay were at high levels among the clergy. It is an extremely competent sociological survey. As the authors are at pains to point out frequently, sociology is not theology. A separate study on the theological aspects of the priesthood was also commissioned. The report of the first commission was not endorsed by the bishops. In the NORC study, the nature of the priesthood, which is our topic, is not precisely mentioned. But many of the chapters, such as "The Spiritual Life of Priests," "Attitudes and Values Among the Catholic Clergy," "Satisfactions and Frustrations in the Priesthood," "The Celibacy Issue," and "Future Plans," do have meaning for our study, as they would have for historical theology.

I chose to depict a typical priest of 1970 from among the middle-aged group in the NORC tables, i.e., those between thirty-six and forty-five years old. He would have been born in

1935, just before World War II, attended a pre-Vatican II seminary and been ordained in 1960, when he was twenty-five. In the NORC data, he would have been in the middle; in real life, he would have been somewhat confused and yet not a young radical of the late sixties and early seventies.

By and large, the NORC report found that Catholic priests are not any more or any less deficient in emotional maturity than other groups in American society. They maintain a high degree of personal morale; most of them engage in some form of regular prayer, and a substantial proportion of them have had frequent religious experiences of union with God; there is a fundamental acceptance of basic religious values to which the church is officially committed; they are more "liberal" than the laity on social issues, but less so than bishops. On the other hand, a large number of them are dissatisfied with the way in which the ecclesiastical structure is shaped and the way in which decision-making power is distributed; but the leadership of the church does not share these dissatisfactions. In fact, the differences between priests and bishops were substantial and systematic on almost every issue studied. This was especially true of mandatory celibacy.

Perhaps this point may illustrate a larger issue. A majority of priests in 1970 were opposed to mandatory celibacy, and a majority of that majority believed that the rule would be changed by 1980. In 1970, the researchers themselves believed that the three-percent-per-year rate of resignation would continue. Both predictions have been proven wrong. On the other hand, the 1970 survey debunked some opinions that were very popular at the time, e.g., that the priests who left were those who had not dated as young men, or that the "clerical ghetto" was one of the greatest obstacles to an effective priesthood.

These "errors" are mentioned not in disparagement either of the report—which is quite honest about its own limitations—or of the clergy who responded. They do point out the limitations of this kind of approach. As has been said so often, the teaching of the church is not to be defined by taking a poll, especially among the clergy. However, the attempt to measure things led the researchers to a deep awareness of the difficulties inherent in their limited sociological study. They were constantly forced to revise their suppositions and their techniques of dealing with their "models." They frequently became aware that they had not asked the right questions to elicit the information they desired. And they became more aware of how impossible it was to define terms such as "modern" religious attitudes ("liberal" would have been even harder to define, and more deceptive), "loneliness," "dissatisfaction with the organizational structure." On the last one, it was at least possible to pinpoint the Priests' Senate. So in the realm of applied research, we come up against a mystery factor. It is not a flight from reason to admit such a factor; it is simply a fact of research. Our deficiency of knowledge is not due solely to our lack of proper technique, but to something else.

Perhaps in our story of Father Tom this is illustrated most clearly by a concluding remark in the survey:

> Two variables—recollection of family tension in one's childhood and experience of contact with God—make relatively small but consistent contributions to the explanation of priestly attitudes and behavior. In the explanation of the propensity to stay in the priesthood, they are almost as important as work satisfaction and values, though obviously less important than such powerful predictors as age and desire to marry. . . . That religious experience does contribute positively to work satisfaction, morale, and the desire to remain a priest may not be surprising to priests, but it is still a moderately important discovery for the rather undeveloped tradition of empirical research on mystical experiences.[24]

It was on these basic assumptions that the picture of Father Tom was developed. An interesting update can be found in Andrew Greeley's later *American Catholics Since the Council: An Unauthorized Report* (Chicago: Thomas More Press, 1985). In 1985, Greeley was still concerned about the vocation factor that had emerged in such a depressing way in the NORC report.

"The laity are not about to leave the church. The clergy, however, are in the process of committing collective suicide because
they do not have enough confidence in themselves and their
work to actively recruit young men to follow them into the
priesthood."[25] Greeley's final conclusion brings us back to mystery, or sociological doubt:

> What has gone wrong in the Catholic priesthood in the United
> States since the Second Vatican Council? Even stated as simply
> as that last question, the crisis in the priesthood remains to a
> considerable extent inexplicable. The changes of the Second
> Vatican Council did something to the priesthood from which it
> has yet to recover. Until we understand better than we do now
> why the Council was such a savage blow to the morale, the self-
> esteem, the self-confidence and the self-respect of priests, we
> will have to accept as almost inevitable the continued decline in
> the number of priests available to minister to the church and
> the mounting problems for laity and for priests because of that
> decline.[26]

5. Personal Problems of Priests

A. *The authority structure bothers priests*
on a personal level.
The NORC study reported in its summary:

1. Large numbers of priests are dissatisfied with the way the ecclesiastical structure is shaped and the way decision-making power
   is distributed; but the leadership of the Church does not share
   this dissatisfaction. Furthermore, it would appear that differences
   between younger and older priests on the distribution of power
   and authority are rooted in ideological differences about the
   nature of the Church and religion.
2. There are systematic and substantial differences between bishops
   and priests on almost every matter we studied. In most cases,
   the bishops hold different points of view and positions than even
   the priests in their own age group. Given the disagreements over
   power and over appropriate reforms in the Church, these sys-

tematic differences of conviction indicate a serious and poten-
tially dangerous "gap" between the priests and the hierarchy.[27]

Since 1971 the situation has changed somewhat, although
professional measuring has not been undertaken. Bishops have
become increasingly informal in their approach to priests as well
as in their public presence. Priests' Senates, or a similar structure, have been established in most dioceses. They have not
worked very well for there is some evidence that priests' re-
sentments have turned largely against such bodies. For one
thing, they have been diluted by similar and larger bodies of
laity, sometimes termed "Pastoral Council," among others.
Seemingly working better are an increasing number of social
and spiritual gatherings of priests.

By and large, the situation is probably improving. Robert
Trisco, in the companion volume of *Historical Investigations*, has
a chapter on "Bishops and Their Priests in the United States."[28]
Discord, more than harmony, marked the relations of bishops
and priests during the nineteenth century. We have a long tradition. Apart from personalities, the democratizing of the church
in the United States has been going on for a long time and has
presented a focus of discontent between *Romanita* and indigenous social patterns.

Older priests probably feel the change more keenly. The
older system did work at times. It was an "old boys' network,"
to be sure. But priests knew how it worked. Consultation was
a privilege and was extended on the basis of merit, or at least
on the basis of personal choice by the bishop. One achieved
status and dignity first within a deanery, and the deanery often
worked effectively as a network of parishes. Bishops and su-
periors realized that they could not accomplish much by themselves and that they needed the backing of their colleagues. The
network worked as long as it continually took in neophytes as
"old boys." It trained them in the system, and a certain conti-
nuity resulted in which the rules of the game were known and
accepted. The penalties for breaking the rules were known as

well as the possibilities for getting around them. This began with seminary training and continued for life. It was a system that had fairly well-defined rewards: titles, clerical approval, promotions, awards and increases in financial benefits.

In a way, it was ward politics. We have moved into a larger arena of church politics these days, with conventions and committees and departments, with publicity and media use, with popular support and opposition. We do not yet know how to make these new elements work efficiently within the church, and we are hesitant to admit too openly that they constitute a political power structure. We are caught in the middle of our own democratizing.

B. Loneliness

Perhaps as a corollary of this situation, priests often feel more lonely than ever. Of course there is no reason why they should not feel a certain amount of loneliness. It is part of the human condition, and certainly part of the celibacy factor. Fr. Charles Curran, a psychologist, used to illustrate the value of celibacy by referring to the Great American Western. In innumerable movies, the good guy with the white hat came riding into town, sided with the poor ranchers against the cattle barons, fell in love with the demure daughter of the farmer, shot up the bad guys and "as the sun was sinking slowly in the west," rode out of town—alone. On a deeper plane, many of the saints knew the value and inevitability of loneliness. "You have made our hearts for you and restless are they until they rest in you," said Augustine.

On the human level, however, the social breakdowns after World War II and the reaction against the "clerical ghetto" after Vatican II left many priests without the older support systems that went along with the "old boys' network." Identity and status were lost too rapidly and not replaced by something else. In many dioceses at the present time, new efforts are being made to create "support systems" for priests. Like most idealistic movements, the going is slow and often superficial. The loss of identity is particularly painful to younger priests, and older priests often feel rejected. The matter has not been helped by the occasional feminist who seems to delight in denigrating priests.[29] The pain is sometimes deep.

Added to this is the lack of new vocations. The only apostolic-succession problem that bothers most priests is: Who is going to do my job when I retire? That they themselves may be responsible for the lack of vocations is certainly true. Nonetheless, it increases their sense of loneliness and rejection.

C. Stress

In 1982, the National Council of Catholic Bishops commissioned a study on "Priests and Stress."[30] It gave a lengthy litany of factors that induce stress in priests:

General Environment
    Lack of stability in the world
    Passing of their type of priesthood
    Confusing developments in theology
    Mandatory retirement policies for older priests
    Division over the "social gospel"
    Confusion in areas of sexuality
    Dispensations from marriage obligations
    Issues of authority and obedience
    Precipitous decline in the number of vocations

Expectations and Demands
    Expectations that today's priest possess an incredibly wide range of talents and skills, from theology to management
    Considerable new work, especially in committees
    A sense of urgency in the priest's work
    Professional updating

Lack of Recognition and Support
    Lack of a realistic system of rewards
    Work with polarized communities
    Lack of affirmation from "significant others"

Neglect of Physical Health

Neglect of Emotional Health
Difficulties with Spirituality
    Overcommitment to work
    Inability to accept limitations
    Retreat into sterile professionalism

Such a list could give almost any priest a case of hypochondria, and unjustifiably. As the NORC report indicated, priests are just as mature and stable as the male population at large and have a remarkably high morale.[31] The incidence of alcoholism and psychotic behavior is about the same as in the general population. These disorders need to be treated along with any physical ones they have, and there the incidence is higher. But the basic problem is not with the individual, nor even with the system. It is with the whole of creation. This is what God made. As Jesus said, "I do not ask you to take them out of the world, but to guard them from the evil one" (John 17:15). Perhaps we do not like to admit the earthly realism of those words.

FOUR

Seminaries and the Future

JOE SEMINARIAN

Tom Hurley and Joe Koch were having pizza at the local trattoria of last resort. With a pitcher of beer before them, they were ruefully contemplating the remains of the latest culinary concoction.

"Pretty good," said Joe somewhat dubiously, and since that drew no response, he went on: "How's the rehabbing project coming, Father Tom?"

Tom Hurley was surprised by the "Father." It dawned on him that young seminarians were once again calling him Father. He didn't know if the change was in him or in them. After all, he had passed fifty some few years ago, and he guessed that now he was considered an "old" man. And Joe, one of his protégés, could scarcely be called an adolescent; he was hanging slightly over the thirty fence himself. But Tom resolutely pushed these darkening thoughts away and smiled.

"All right," he said, "except for old Ward Boss Michels himself. He talks and talks and keeps telling me how many important people he's going to get on our side, but nothing ever happens. Those last two houses are still tied up in a dispute with the building commissioner's office. But we'll get them. I have two families that need those houses, and we'll get them in if we have to march the streets and blow the trumpets." He grinned at the conventional picture that came to him ready-made.

Joe laughed. "You know," he said, "that's the thing I like about you. You never seem to run out of enthusiasm for the job. I don't know if I could ever be as excited about all these social-betterment plans you have, but I admire you for it. When are you going to grow old?"

Tom made a note that it wasn't he who was doing most of the changing. "I like being a priest," he said. "How about you? How did the first year at the seminary go?"

"Once I got in, it wasn't bad," Joe replied. "Getting in was almost as tough as applying for a job with the FBI. I thought you would just write a letter or so and that would be that. But by the time I dealt with the vocation office, hung out with the associates program for a year, was analyzed and purified by the vocation director and the staff psychologist, and checked off on the diagnostic list by academic deans, formation teams and the rector, I began to feel like that old-time computer card—bent, stapled and torn. Mighty powerful corporation we have here."

Tom chuckled and remembered some of his more-recent experiences with the chancery office, which seemed to be the greatest growth industry in the diocese. "Keeps them busy and in a job," he observed.

"Oh, it's not all that bad, and I suppose it has its merits. By the end of the year, I was beginning to see some sense in it."

"What are you the most interested in, Joe?" asked Father Tom. "Why do you want to be a priest?"

"Right now I want to get a solid theological foundation.

Mainly, I'm interested in courses on spirituality. They tell me there used to be more of them in the curriculum, but there are still a good number. And they have some good people, old smiling Art and Jeannie. The way I see it now, I'm going to affect people more by what I am than by what I do. I used to think that the spiritual stuff was window-dressing for the sake of the customers, but I don't look at it that way any more. If you ask me what's important, I'd say prayer and holiness, and a sense of responsibility, which I don't really have a lot of as yet."

"Whatever happened to all the funny Masses?" Tom asked sudenly, for no good reason that he could identify.

"Funny Masses?"

"Yes, you know, balloons and Indian vestments, readings from John Cheever, and the Top Ten for music. I thought I heard that the real thing was a Mass celebrated in the rec hall with baked-ham sandwiches."

"Never heard of it," said Joe. "We like liturgy to be liturgy. Keep it moving, but keep it dignified." And then in a fearful voice of confession, he added, "We sometimes have Benediction."

"Well, that's a heresy," Tom said with a laugh. "What are you going to do about it after you're ordained?"

"Oh, I think I'll see it as the church. There's a fine phrase we keep hearing about creating community. I'm not sure what it means, but it's better than saying 'building church,' much better than saying 'building a church.' I think of all those people out there wandering around in different stages of spiritual development. Something has to draw them together so they can discover the other side of life. I kind of see myself as the one who does the drawing together."

Since this was getting rather preachy, Tom took off on another tack. "How's Carol?" he asked.

"Great girl, that," Joe said. "She's got herself a new boyfriend. I learned a lot from her. Not that way," he smiled. "She's a real lady. And she understands."

"Why didn't you marry her?" prodded Tom.

"I don't really know," Joe replied. "I guess I was in love with her. But it just didn't seem to jell. And then there was this other nagging conviction that I was cut out to be something different. Maybe I'm deceiving myself with the romantic idea of being the guy on the white horse who sets everything straight and then rides out as the sun slowly sets in the west. But it was there. She said to me one night, 'Joe, I appreciate you and like you. But you love something or somebody else and I know I could never have you completely. You're going to have to settle that first.' "

"Doesn't the celibacy thing bother you?" asked Tom.

"Sure. It bothers everybody, I presume. How do I know what I will be ten or twenty years from now? Look at you. You're a happy priest. How did you make it? If you can do it, so can I."

Tom smiled to himself. He appreciated the compliment, and he was amused at the self-certainty of the young, or at least of the inexperienced. He knew the price he had paid, the wrenching shift from his own pre-Vatican II beginnings, his idealism, his despondency and frustration, and now his somewhat precarious acceptance. Even that caused him some mirth. Looking at this younger man who admired him, he realized how much he had been disturbed by trying to be like someone else. He was both too old and too young. His present enthusiasms for helping others seemed at times like a race to keep up with the seventies and arriving after the race was over. On the other hand, he seemed prematurely old and wise when he didn't feel old or wise at all.

"You know," he said apropos of nothing as he pushed his plate away, "I don't think I like pizza."

REFLECTIONS

The picture of Joe Seminarian was drawn from the Hemrick-Hoge report of 1985 (*Seminarians in Theology: A National Pro-*

file, by Eugene F. Hemrick and Dean R. Hoge, Washington, D.C.: USCC, June, 1985, sponsored by the Bishops' Committee on Priestly Formation, the National Conference of Catholic Bishops, the National Catholic Educational Association, and the Assembly of Ordinaries and Rectors/Presidents of Theologates). The study was based on the return of over three thousand questionnaires from seminarians in theology. It was intended to update a previous study made by CARA in 1966–67 and entitled: *Seminarians of the Sixties.* This research is not as in-depth as the NORC report on priests that was used in the previous chapter.

Relevant to our investigation, the Hemrick-Hoge report offered the following summary conclusions on page 2:

- The two most influential factors causing seminarians to become priests are an inner calling and a priest's example.
- Being prayerful is the most important quality seminarians point to for any religious ministry. Second is being able to relate to people.
- The most important activity in any religious ministry is building community, with preaching ranking second.
- Holiness is seen as the most important quality a priest can possess, with apostolic zeal ranking a distant second.
- Preaching and teaching are seen as the most important activities a priest can be involved in, with celebrating the sacraments a close second.
- Responsibility ranks first and apostolic zeal second as the most important qualities seminarians feel they need.
- In carrying out parish work, seminarians see the function of the liturgy and sacramental ministry as most essential.

Throughout the study, references are made to changes that have taken place since 1966. "Since 1966 there has been increased emphasis on sacraments and decreased emphasis on witness to the world. Also, the emphasis on counseling has weakened since 1966" (page 26). In the final "Questions Needing Discussion," the researchers, who are themselves middle-aged men, ask:

"Should we have expected that social justice does not rank high with seminarians? Are we in an age in the American church in which seminarians should become more sensitive to social justice?" (page 47). The shift in seminarians' attitudes on the crucial questions of spirituality and social activism has been most notable to we who have been engaged in seminary work for a good number of years.

The picture drawn in this chapter attempts to pit the average seminarian of today against a priest who would have been his peer before Vatican II and went through the trauma. For this purpose, Father Tom, the Statistic, was used from the previous chapter.

Whatever this small vignette may say, I hope it suggests that with seminarians there is no simple trajectory from "conservative" to "liberal," whatever those words may mean to the reader, from "old" to "new," from "dull" to "exciting." Some old things keep emerging in the priesthood even when we do not foster them. Some problems keep popping up and we do not know why. The Hemrick-Hoge report certainly does not ask all the questions we would like to have answered; the authors themselves suggest that more research be done. But there is also a sneaking suspicion that we may never know.

1. Introduction

When I was ordained, I was assigned to teach in a seminary. By the time I was fifteen years ordained, I thought I knew how to run one. So I became a rector for the first time. I remember that I confidently announced to myself, and probably to the community as well, that with three hundred years of experience behind my community and with my great personal preparation, we were quite ready to handle the situation. Five years later I was willing to admit to more problems than I had anticipated. And five years after that, when I was a provincial and in the midst of the Vatican II change, I was willing to admit that I did not know very much at all.

Left: One Mile Tavern which became the Seminary of St. Sulpice (St. Mary's Seminary, Baltimore), the first U.S. seminary.

(Sulpician Archives, Baltimore)

(St. Thomas Seminary Archives)

Seminary classrooms look differently in the '80s. St. Thomas Seminary, Denver.

Fr. Dennis Comey of the Institute of Industrial Relations at St. Joseph's College, Philadelphia, addressing workingmen during the Depression.

(Our Sunday Visitor)

In the fifties a typical faculty and student photograph looked formidable. St. Thomas Seminary, Denver.

Graduation classes at seminaries look differently in recent years. St. Thomas Seminary, Denver, 1986.

The traditional "graduation" in semi-naries was ordination. Archbishop Francis Stafford and Fr. Marcus Madrano, 1986.

(The Denver Catholic Register)

Pope John Paul II and Fr. Ernesto Cardenal, Culture Minister of Nica-ragua, in a dispute over political involvement.

(AP/Wide World Photos, Inc.)

Fr. Tim Dempsey was the very model of the Irish priest. St. Louis, 1920s.

(Missouri Historical Society)

Thomas Aquinas

Vincent de Paul

Charles Borromeo

Augustine

(Sketches by Kathleen Rose)

Life, however, does not change completely every five or
ten years. The present is building on the past however much
we indulge in the rhetoric of change. Now, an additional twenty
years later, I can see how slow and reluctant we were to change,
and how foolish we were to make so many changes simply to
keep up with the enthusiasms of the time. Meanwhile, we are
at the beginning of another change. Sometimes it seems that
we are in the recycling business. A good number of the young
(and some of the middle-aged) are going back to pre-Vatican
II attitudes and policies, sometimes to those we had hoped to
eradicate. That frightens me. However, I also see many of the
middle-aged liberals now in charge behaving as though times
had not changed in the past twenty years. That frightens me
even more. Meanwhile I have learned to a certain extent that
the changes which I approved and which were effected did prove
satisfying, but it was sometimes those which I did not which
contributed most to growth.

2. The Changes

Reciting the statistics of change is a fairly easy procedure since
we have so much research on seminaries.[1] To take a few convenient figures: In 1966, there were 8,916 students in theological seminaries; in 1984, there were 6,261.[2] In 1966, there
were 133 theological seminaries; in 1984, there were 57. Almost half of the schools, most of them run by religious communities, have merged. Some of those have formed clusters, or
consortia; a few of them have merged with universities, although
that is a rarer pattern. The great majority of students are still
educated in freestanding seminaries. Meanwhile, the number
of nonclerical students has increased from extremely few in
1966 to an estimated twenty-percent full-time students, or approximately thirty-three percent if the part-time students are
counted; in some seminaries they outnumber the clerical students. By 1983, women students comprised approximately nine

percent. Seventy percent of the seminaries were admitting non-priesthood candidates to graduate programs.

Equally significant, the cost per year of educating these students has gone up from $10,082 in 1979, when we first began to compile expense figures nationwide, to $13,135 by 1985.[3] Although this is in line with the costs of American higher education, it is a shock to those who pay the bills (or don't). Only about one-third of this cost is paid by way of tuition; the rest must be made up from subsidies contributed by dioceses, religious communities or development funds; the latter are becoming increasingly important. Much of this money goes into paying administrative costs and lay faculty. Lay faculty has grown from an occasional person to perhaps one third of all faculty.

The faculty has also changed. In 1966, the majority of faculty members (and administrators) were priests. We have no precise figures, but it is probable that the number of faculty and administrative personnel, full- and part-time, has doubled since 1966. The faculty is certainly better prepared degree-wise than in 1966; there are many more doctorates and double degrees. Many of the present faculty are lay. By 1984, women made up sixteen percent of the full-time faculty. Many faculty members have degrees from universities other than the traditional ecclesiastical schools.[4]

Unchanged is the way in which the "system," if it can be called that, is financed. In the first period of seminary expansion, seminaries were founded and funded (poorly) by dioceses and religious communities. In the diocesan scene, as new dioceses were split off, the better-established mother diocese usually offered to continue educating seminarians free of charge. It is only within the past fifty years or less that tuition and room and board has been charged, and then it has usually been only a token sum, designed to attract less-affluent students. However, today the system is so entrenched that the client dioceses consider themselves customers and they shop for the lower prices. Currently the sponsoring diocese is burdened with the cost of educating the priests of other dioceses, and resistance to spreading the expenses equitably is extremely high. The problem was first openly discussed by a small number of bishops at a meeting in Chicago in 1982, but nothing has been done about it to date. It is one of the glaring inequities in the administration of the Catholic Church in the United States. Obviously this is a national problem, but it is refused a national hearing.

Academics has changed greatly in the past twenty years. In 1968, Catholic theological seminaries began a general move for accreditation by the Association of Theological Schools. ATS is an accrediting agency of professional schools on a par with other professional associations that certify law schools, engineering schools, medical schools and so forth. By 1984, forty-nine out of fifty-seven seminaries were so accredited; many are also accredited by regional associations such as the Middle States Association and the North Central Association. In other words, Catholic seminaries are on a par with American education in general. The cry to "join the mainstream of American education," which was so often voiced just after Vatican II, has now largely been met, at least on paper.

The method of classroom teaching has also changed greatly. Before 1966, American seminaries were heavy on textbooks and theological manuals, often written in Latin. Today the prevailing modus operandi is discussion centered on a wide variety of readings. Emphasis is placed on the methodology of investigation. Before 1966, the curriculum was largely set by the school; the student had few choices to make except among peripheral courses such as languages and pastoral specialties. Now most seminaries offer electives and even a choice of degree programs (usually a Master of Arts of some sort), although the Master of Divinity degree is normally considered a requirement for ordination. Field education is an accepted component of all seminary curricula. Internships are virtually as common. Many students also take courses at institutions that have working agreements with seminaries. The old charge that seminaries are closed-in academic institutions has little validity today.

There are pluses and minuses to be found here. Faculty

degrees and publication have been strengthened; whether teaching skills have been improved is unknown. But then it is unknown in most educational institutions; it is a component that escapes measurement. The curriculum has become more flexible and, we hope, more relevant. On the other hand, seminarians have lost much of the integration that resulted from the fixed curricula. The concept of theology as an academic discipline has been diluted in favor of keeping students informed as to what is current. Along with the decrease in academic discipline has come a more general loss of discipline in the sense of learning the tools of a trade and sticking to a task until it is done. There is an understandable trade-off involved here, but students themselves today say that the thing they need most is a sense of responsibility.[5]

Formation has also changed. Spirituality is a major concern of seminarians of the eighties, but it is not as unadulterated as is the traditional spirituality. Much of it has a psychological basis. In fact, the model often seems more psychological than ascetical.[6] Seminarians themselves sense this.[7]

There is a disturbing note in all this change. As the impact of Vatican II swept through the seminaries, many of the older professors were not able to stand the pressure for change; they retired prematurely or simply gave up trying to steer the course in which they believed. The younger men who were pushing for change were in the age group that suffered the most resignations, both from teaching and from the priesthood. Thus the normal accretion of maturing and responsible administrators was interrupted. Young men had to be advanced rapidly, forgoing the usual experience of coming up slowly through the ranks. They were forced to experiment and to make decisions without the benefit of mature counsel. We are only gradually recovering from a generation gap in administrative personnel.[8]

Students are changing. One measurable area is that of age; the average age of theology students has gone up by about three years since 1965. Three age categories are almost equally represented: early to mid-twenties; mid-twenties to thirty; thirty-one and over.[9] On the other hand, seminaries have not been flooded with older entrants. Nor has the more experienced seminarian lived up to the expectancies placed on him by the facts of his maturity and his previous career. The old accusation that seminarians never had the experience of dating girls does not seem to hold water.[10]

By and large, the older candidates are indistinguishable from the younger except for their greater participation in church life as deacons or members of parish councils before entrance into the seminary.[11] The debit has been that older men change less. Seminarians often exhibit the same tendencies to be followers rather than leaders that were criticized in an early day. Broader personal freedom has often increased their awareness of the weakness of their self-image. The psychological services now offered in seminaries have resulted not simply from choice, but from need. Moreover, although seminaries stress the necessity for leadership qualities, nobody in the church is able to define exactly what is meant by this. Leadership comes in many sizes and shapes. Some are appropriate and some are not; being a gang leader obviously is not. But what is? Our clichés do not stretch very far.

Then there are those qualities in students that have not changed very much or perhaps are being recycled. The strongest nationalities of seminarians are still found among the Irish, German, Austrian, Dutch and Swiss; Hispanics are greatly underrepresented.[12] Seminarians come from average-sized Catholic families, and most of them have Catholic parents who attend Mass regularly.[13] The majority of seminarians have been altar servers.[14] In general, the background of seminarians has changed little. They still come from middle-class, stable families with average education. Those who come from seminary colleges have a higher rate of perseverance and greater certitude about their vocational commitment.[15]

Their attitudes are also middle-of-the-road. They think that prayerfulness is the most important quality for a religious ministry. They see building community and preaching as important.

In parish work they see liturgy and sacramental ministry as most essential.[16] They also believe that helping others will be their most rewarding experience, but it should be noted that more diocesan seminarians in 1984 rated celebrating the sacraments above helping others than did their counterparts in 1966.[17] As noted previously, the middle-aged compilers of the report were surprised at this. It gave rise to an unusual incursion of editorializing in the report. It is not clear whether this is a commentary on the seminarians or on the pollsters.

Those of us who work in seminaries are in daily touch with these findings from sociological studies and perhaps we give somewhat different weight to various elements within them, although we would surely agree that the polls are eliciting authentic information. There are those subtle things we notice. Despite the departure of cassock and surplice, students still gravitate at times to the high-priestly style in liturgy. "Hall Masses," or small group liturgies, are out; guitars are not essential; Benediction is even celebrated. Students are known to dress up for formal occasions; they have been heard to address priests as "Father." In the early morning or late at night, some of them can be seen quietly meditating in chapel; they do not need pressurized sensitivity sessions to discover the "real me," as did the youths of the sixties.

Behind this is something to which only long years of closeness and comparison can sensitize one. In many ways these students are still the same as the students of fifty years ago. There is a mystique, an idealism, that is not purely natural, a desire for a challenge that would escape many others. There is the mystery of it all. They still retain a sense of difference and separateness. They have heard and seen demonstrated the theories that they are just another minister in the church. They are not buying. Perhaps the price is too high; celibacy, poverty and obedience are worth too much. They are not opting for the easy solutions. The clothes have changed, and indeed, the man has changed. But the priesthood still exerts a pull on these young students that is beyond rational explanation.

3. Problems

Probably one of the most pressing needs in the church today is for a national policy on the basics of seminary education in the United States. The woeful neglect of a national policy on who pays for what has been noted above. The problem will not go away, and it is more determinative of seminary existence than most bishops or Catholics in general would care to admit. So the CARA-Lilly study.[18] However, there are other problems equally as pressing. The recruitment and placement of students in seminaries is now on a free-market basis. The pool of prospects is apparently well limited. Who gets whom? Many seminaries have instituted recruiting programs of their own, placing themselves in competition with other seminaries equally in need of a suitably sized student body. Much time and money is spent, none of which is increasing the total number of entrants on a national level. In the founding days, when new dioceses were being offered practically free education, seminaries were at least committed to supporting specific institutions with the bulk of their prospects, and seminaries could do some sensible planning. Now an individual seminary is at the mercy of students and vocation directors, who have a free choice. They owe no allegiance to anyone, and often decisions are made on the basis of personal taste or satisfaction.

In a way, the real accrediting agencies today are the vocation directors. No one wants to lock individuals into a rigid system, but obviously the lack of a national policy of some sort is deleterious to seminaries. Far worse is the ecclesiology that seems to lie behind the process. Instead of a catholic concept of a federation of helping churches, we now have a free-enterprise system of gross capitalism that says: Let those who do not compete for our favors go out of business. There must be a better way of looking at national needs than this.

Despite these debilitating factors that often sap the enthusiasm and threaten the security of faculty and students in individual seminaries, there is actually more commonality at work in seminaries than ever before. In previous days it came from religious communities, which gave a common stamp to the institutions they ran; today it comes from national organizations, even those that are voluntary. On an official level, Rome has mandated general policies and the NCCB has formulated the "Program for Priestly Formation," which lays down general guidelines for all seminaries in the country.[19] Although various models are permitted, these guidelines have given a certain uniformity to seminary education in the United States. To one who visits half a dozen or more seminaries, or to one who works in a seminary, an unofficial but certain homogeneity may be discernible. One knows beforehand that there will be a midday liturgy, that there are cafeteria lines and a laundromat, that the student parking lot is extensive and that there will be many secretaries.

The recent visitation of seminaries mandated by Pope John Paul II was made possible by the commonality that exists. The visitations were carried out by personnel from among the bishops, provincials and seminary faculties themselves according to guidelines devised in the U.S. The initial summary from the Sacred Congregation of Education concerning freestanding seminaries presumed a common model that the visitors had in mind and a de facto commonality on which they were able to measure success. Although no one knows the further uses that will be made of this report, it is quite clear from what has already been said that certain parameters are being drawn.[20]

In addition to these official acts that move seminaries toward a common pattern, there is a voluntary networking. The National Catholic Educational Association has for many years had a seminary department; indeed, this department predated the NCEA. At one time it was hoped that the NCEA might grow into a professional accrediting association, with a center at Catholic University of America. This and an even earlier move to have all seminaries accredited to the Catholic University of America never caught on with many seminaries. Yet the NCEA acts as a powerful informational and educational source through its publications, "Seminaries in Dialogue" and "Seminary Newsletter," and increasingly through the sociological research it sponsors such as the CARA-Lilly report on finances and the Hemrick-Hoge report on "Seminarians in Theology."

The center of seminary innovation lies no longer with Sulpicians, Vincentians and Benedictines, but with the NCCB. Then there are regional associations such as the Midwest Association of Theological Schools (an in-house Catholic organization) and the informal annual meetings of the Midwest and Eastern rectors and various other officers. Seminaries constitute a "system" now more than ever before. No one in these voluntary organizations is trying to subdue individuality or experimentation in seminaries, but the very fact that seminaries need to huddle together for protection inevitably makes for a certain commonality.

4. The Prospects

What lies ahead? Any seminary rector would dearly love to know, but there are no tea leaves. Everyone in the know is aware that the great problem is ecclesiology. Which way will the grass-roots church go? In this country, seminaries have followed need, not created options. Will the church follow the equality of the all-the-baptized model, or will it find some new way of activating the hierarchical model? There are real cutting edges to these supposedly abstract questions. What view do seminaries with many lay students take toward those students who earn equally authenticated Master of Divinity degrees but are not priests?

The recent letter of the Sacred Congregation noted: "Seminaries are established by the Church for the particular purpose of training candidates for the priesthood. The life-style has a specific character, and studies are undertaken with a specific end in view. The participation in classes and lectures of people who are not themselves candidates for the priesthood may be welcomed in small number, provided that their different vocational needs be respected, and that the central purpose for which the seminary exists be not weakened."[21] This is not simply a "backward Roman view"; the Midwest rectors in 1984 wrote: "The local church should assume the primary responsibility for those other ministerial training programs. The seminary should be willing to lend its resources to collaborating with others who direct these programs."[22] The experience of these men who had run seminaries consisting of a good number of lay students indicated to them that a seminary should not attempt to be an all-purpose school of ministry. The concern for a distinctive priestly formation still rests on our developing understanding of ecclesiology.

The financial burden of seminaries lays a heavy obligation on the local administration. Many rectors and treasurers are not professionally prepared for this. It is easy to suggest that we should either provide professional training for the priests who do the job or hire lay professionals. However, the matter is not that simple. Priests who earn degrees in administration or finance have not been honed by the rough and tumble of the business world; if we hire lay professionals, we make a distinction between administration and formation. Administration is an important part of the future shape of the church. It cannot be easily separated from the whole concept of priestly authority, nor can it be separated from the concept of church leadership. One cannot avoid the dictum that "he who controls the purse strings controls the organization." This too is governed by spiritual principles, not simply by professionalism. Modeling priesthood for candidates embraces administration and finance. We are in a financial crisis of some magnitude with our seminaries; the problem needs to be solved, but just how is not clear.

Faculty is another problem. The number of qualified and competent (there is a difference) priests who can teach in seminaries is declining. Up to the present, the number of seminaries has decreased sufficiently that this has not become critical. However, we do not know if sufficient numbers of those who will be willing to undertake the task are being prepared for it. We have no research on this question. Moreover, as seminaries have hired lay faculty, they have discovered a whole new source of supply. It is too early to tell the future of this practice. It takes several years to discover whether or not a person with a degree is a good seminary professor. The pay is certainly not a great enticement. Up to the present, we seem to have discovered that there are sufficient lay people with high ideals who are willing to make a financial sacrifice. Most of them are part-time teachers who do not need to rely solely on the seminary system for their total career. But we do not know how far back the pipeline extends. If it continues as it is at present, we are probably not in trouble.

Vocations are the most obvious controlling factor of the future. Our research indicates that the decline in the number of prospects entering theological seminaries as priesthood students has leveled off.[23] Sociological research further indicates that the suasion of another priest and the influence of a mother are still the crucial factors in vocations. Research also indicates that the idealism behind individual vocations has not changed much. The young are attracted to a career that is challenging, mysterious and service-oriented. The principal deterrents at present are lifelong commitment and, in some way, celibacy, although it is not quite clear to what degree the latter is a critical issue.

It would be a rather inexperienced person who would venture to make any long-term predictions on future trends. Beyond the students who are already in the pipeline, statistics cannot help us much. Those of us who lived through pre- and post-Vatican II know how unpredictable statistics are. Andrew Greeley concluded recently that as a sociologist he simply did not understand either the decline in vocations or the dropping out of so many priests.[24]

Seminarians in Theology concluded that "the following matters will influence the choice of young Catholics in coming years to become priests or not:

- the increasing number of ministries

- feminist pressures for the ordination of women
- mandatory celibacy for the clergy
- the decreasing number of religious
- the evolving nature of the parish and the evolving roles for the priest in it
- the growth of shared responsibility for parish and diocesan administration
- changes in the ethnic culture of the Catholic Church (especially the growth of the Hispanic Catholic population)

The data that are presented here say nothing about these questions."[25]

One cannot add up uncertain pluses or minuses, nor can one predict a future from the survey figures cited above. They are simply parts of a whole and there may be others that are equally, if not more, important.

One thing seems to have remained constant, however, at least to the present, Bishops, who are the real customers for priests, still put their first emphasis on holiness. They may have all kinds of hopes and desires for an "exciting" or a "solid" presbyterate, but they will settle for holy men. They agree with the seminarians. Just what this means is rather vague, but it does project an image. The danger to it is one this book has frequently mentioned and will do so again, namely, that priestly formation will become a one-issue program. That issue is likely to be professionalism. Pushed to an extreme, that determines the ecclesiology that one espouses.

Despite the conventional wisdom (or folly), seminaries have never existed in a vacuum. American seminary education has always been extremely pragmatic. It has served the church very well in past times when social conditions within and without the Catholic Church were quite different than today's. If seminaries were isolated, so were Catholics. If seminaries were largely dedicated to teaching discipline, so were the immigrants. So also today seminaries reflect the temper of the Catholic population. If there is confusion in seminaries, there is confusion in parishes. If leadership among faculty, administration and student body is uncertain, so is it in the broader church.

We do not call seminaries parishes or think of what goes on in them as pastoral activity. But that is the case. Seminary rectors would rather think of themselves as pastors than as administrators, as would good faculty members. Seminaries are not segregated, exclusive societies—clerical clubs—separate from the church. The clergy exist for the church. Even the most benighted conservative knows that.

FIVE
What Makes Father Run?

1. Introduction

This chapter might more appropriately be entitled "The Spirituality of the American Priest." However, that sounds rather remote and esoteric. The basic question is: Why do priests continue to live and act as priests in America today? And why should young men enter the priesthood? The wonder is not that there are so few of them, but that there are any. They know the conditions under which they will pledge their word. Whatever the various prophets may claim for the future, these young men must live in the present parameters of the existing discipline. Why? What makes Father run?

What are the roots for such action, and what are the current hopes amid the problems? Granted that there are extremists to the right and to the left, and granted that there are independent characters who would not fit any pattern, the next questions are: What is the mainstream telling us about the spirituality of priests? And how can we honestly clarify our present direction?

123

Here the tie-in with previous considerations is the word "mystery." We are not dealing with a faraway mystery, but one embedded in the daily and total American life. It should be apparent by now that by spirituality I mean the basic motivations founded on faith and encompassing a segment of human experience that lead men to live as they do. This is not the same as theology or the history of theology; those involve an intellectual attempt to state historically what is in the deposit of faith and the development of doctrine. Throughout this book I have tried to point out that the question of spirituality is not one of ivory-tower thinking; it grows out of lived situations. However, it is not immediately spirituality. The sociological thread tries to tie the abstractions to the living reality, but that also is not spirituality. Finally, there is psychology, which can be probed empirically to a certain extent, although its conclusions depend on somewhat uncertain premises of what lies behind the manifestations it attempts to describe. That also is not spirituality, although today it is sometimes passed off as such. All of this is important for understanding the present situation, and we have dealt with it in a somewhat cursory fashion.

However, we are still engaged in a study of data that lies within the purview of empirical evidence. We now need to probe those more hidden areas of knowledge and motivation, made partly of clay and partly of blood, to paraphrase Daniel. Spirituality also has its own history, although it is not one of tidy cause and effect. It also expresses itself in images that are found both in the literature and in the people. There is a vast library of such writings, ranging from John Chrysostom to the latest NCCB treatise, entitled *As One Who Serves*.[1]

2. A Brief History of Priestly Spirituality

The earliest pictures of priests that emerge in our history reveal something of the motivation that led men to seek out and try to live the vocation. Early on, the Old Testament begins to exert its influence by supplying images not as structural imperatives, but as motives. Fathers such as John Chrysostom, Theodore of Mopsuestia, Cassidus, Hesychias, Cyril of Alexandria and Denis seemed to center the image around the distinction of being set apart, the duty of confrontation and the dignity of the sacred.

As the church became legitimatized in the fourth century and shortly afterward took over many of the organizational functions of the state, the ideal priest was viewed as someone like Ambrose, who stood at the beginning of the period as an administrator. Accompanying the image was the monastic ideal, which spread rapidly throughout the West and became the preservator of so many traditions of the culture within minisocieties. *"Ora et labora"*—"Pray and work"—became the ideal. Monks and priests did just that while fostering agriculture, learning and discipline, and providing people with splendid liturgy.

The medieval priest also had his place embedded in society. He was part of the feudal system, ideally working behind the scenes but always providing wise guidance. Learning was expected of him, although in actuality as time went on, a great cleavage developed between the well-educated upper clergy and the hardly educated lower clergy. The medieval universities emerged first of all as schools of theology, and they have left us a great wealth of theological learning, especially in the works of Thomas Aquinas, Bonaventure, Albert and Duns Scotus. Like universities since then, they provided the escalator to the controlling positions in society. Clerical education at this level eventually tended to become more a matter of job opportunities than of a vocation of service.

Catherine of Siena saw the priest as the visible Christ. Dignity was still important, but what Catherine had to say bore on the responsibility to live up to it. She saw God as demanding charity, purity, service and generosity. Her view was much more ascetical than triumphalistic.

After the Reformation, the ideal changed again. Perhaps

Charles Borromeo was as real a version of the reformed Catholic priest as one can find. However, most of the motivation came from the French school of the seventeenth century. Cardinal De Berulle was the theoretician of French spirituality. In his view, all Christians are called upon to surrender to Jesus in his "states." Priesthood is a "state" and demands that a person come to it by abnegation, doing away with his sinful state and thus being reduced to nothingness. Once in this situation, he is able to "adhere" to the "state" of Jesus, which is permanently that of sacrificial dying. Indifference and adherence to Jesus the Sacrificer are the main characteristics of the French school.[2]

Vincent de Paul, as we shall note more fully later, was attracted to this spirituality, but with a different twist. Vincent founded a community that he called the Congregation of the Mission. By "mission" he did not mean foreign missions, or even home missions. He meant that each priest had a mission to perform for Jesus Christ, and that mission was to make the redemptive work of Jesus the central vision in everyone's life. It was this sort of view that led to the foundation of many later religious communities.

In pre-Vatican II days, the popular piety of the priest, as chronicled in numerous books of spiritual reading, tended to center on a very Thomistic concept of the apartness of the priest, the dignity of the ordination rite itself, and the need for conforming to the state of perfection in which Jesus had placed him.

Popular novels tended to portray priests sympathetically. The priest was someone different, a compassionate shepherd to the weak, a fighter for the oppressed, a martyr to a cause. Any cursory acquaintance with contemporary novels or films will reveal how different the present approach is. Now the priest is the subject of his own weakness.[3]

Vatican II, in its "Decree on the Ministry and Life of Priests," began with a treatment on the nature of the priesthood and the basic functions of priests, both sacramental and in relationship to others in the church, and then considered the "Life of the Priest."[4] The first two sections were strictly theological and bore such headings as "A Priest's Call to Perfection," "Special Spiritual Requirements in the Life of a Priest" and "Helps for the Priest's Life." The first section was a rather conventional statement of the source of special obligations beyond those entailed by baptism. "Priests are bound by a special reason to acquire this perfection. They are consecrated to God in a new way in their ordination and are made living instruments of Christ the eternal priest and so are enabled to accomplish throughout all time that wonderful work of his which with eternal efficacy restored the whole human race" (#12). This core statement is right out of the priestly spirituality of the French school. It has been shifted from Berulle's contemplation of the holiness of God toward Vatican II's own vision of service of the people. "By this grace the priest, through his service of the people committed to his care and all the People of God, is better able to pursue the perfection of Christ, whose place he takes"(#12).

The document then goes on to talk about the ministry of the Eucharist, the other sacraments and the care of the flock. Humility and obedience are singled out as preeminent virtues (#15). The document reaffirms celibacy and poverty as needed witness virtues. In the final section on "Helps for the Priest's Life," it zeroes in on daily prayer, study, honest pay and social security. This is a somewhat odd mixture of ancient themes and contemporary needs.

In general, the Council was following a path that had been well worn in previous generations. While it tried to pay attention to the contemporary concerns of priests and to its own emphasis on the People of God and the mission to the world, these were low-key issues. In a modest way, it was developmental. What it left unsaid was either encouragement or admonition for those more-radical models of priestly life who were so prominent in the sixties.

In 1973, the American bishops issued their own statement

on *Spiritual Renewal of the American Priesthood.*⁵ This was a well-thought-out and relevant pamphlet. It began with—and continued to stress—the theme we treated in the last chapter, namely that the priest lives amidst mystery. His spirituality is the experience of the death-resurrection of Jesus in the ministry and within the American culture. The Statement recognized the obvious characteristics of American culture, both good and bad, both the self-seeking aspirations and the dynamics of abounding life. It used previous research commissioned by the bishops to note the problems, theological as well as psychological, within the priesthood and urged integration of priestly spirituality on the basis of interaction among priests and laity. The Statement deserved more attention than it received, although it certainly played a part in encouraging the growth of programs for bringing priests together more often for spiritual sharing.

3. The Spirituality of American Seminaries

The earliest American seminary was established in 1791, when a small band of Suplicians came from Canada to establish St. Mary's Seminary in Baltimore. The motivation was clear: America needed native priests. It has been a rather consistent policy of the Catholic Church in any missionary country to pave the way for indigenous priests. It is also inevitable that in the early stage the indigenization does not take place very well. The teachers are colonizers to some extent, even when they try their best not to be. Early American seminaries looked very much like their European counterparts; the French and Irish who dominated in the control of seminaries were not particularly friendly to American ideals of liberty and fraternity. Yet inevitably the native culture did shape the design; so also did the lack of adequate financing in the early American seminaries. Most of them were run on a shoestring. As late as 1850, the preparation for priesthood often consisted of no more than one year of philosophy and two years of theology.[6] Medical schools did not demand much more than that for doctors.

The French ideal of the priest was that of a holy man. Even with the modest level of education that the resources of most dioceses would allow for, the clergy were still above competition from lay people in theological education. The American frontier was sufficiently vital for the next hundred years to shape the ideal priest as a tough man able to cope not only with physical deprivation, but with an ever-fractious congregation as the tide of immigrants swept into the hinterland. During the days of the gold rush in Colorado, there were pastors in Leadville who carried a gun and established a modicum of law and order. It was all in a day's work.

In the early 1800s, seminaries were established in remote towns such as Bardstown, Kentucky, and Perryville, Missouri, to minister to areas on the frontier; strong ethnic groups—the Germans in Milwaukee and Columbus, Ohio, for example—demanded seminaries. Later on, especially after the Third Council of Baltimore in 1884 gave a new impetus to improved seminary education, seminaries were established in centers such as New York, Boston, St. Paul, Rochester, San Francisco and St. Louis. The need was for priests who could minister to a burgeoning population and an immense geographic expansion.

The numerous ethnic minorities also imposed upon the priest a good deal of the image he had to carry. If the Irish pastor in Boston or Chicago became virtually a ward boss, that was what his constituency demanded. If the Polish and Slavs in the steel mills had aggressive, activist priests, it was because they were aggressive themselves. If the Germans wanted law and order and German sermons, that determined the kind of priest the church had to supply. The one constant in this was that the priest should be a "holy" man and not disgrace the church with public scandal. Almost anything else could be tolerated.

The image of the American priest has often been denounced as being "anti-intellectual."[7] The earliest seminary faculties were often drawn from highly educated Europeans. After that the brute expansion of the Catholic populace and the lack of sufficient funding tended to reduce seminaries to practical training centers. It is, of course, impossible to predict how the American church would have fared had its energies been diverted into scholarship instead of into trying to keep up with the brute expansion of the Catholic populace.

At any rate, the general trend of the first hundred and fifty years of spiritual formation in American seminaries fell under the influence of the French school dominated by the Sulpicians and Vincentians, who ran most of the diocesan seminaries. Diocesan priests who conducted seminaries generally adhered to the program that was, after all, strongly supported by Rome.

Jesuits, who had such a great impact on Catholic higher education, withdrew early from this apostolate. Between 1833 and 1852 they opened diocesan seminaries in New York and Mobile. As with most seminaries of the time, it was necessary to employ the older students to teach in the lower grades of the colleges attached to seminaries for lay students. The Jesuits decided that this was cutting too deeply into the higher education of their own future, which they quite rightly saw as in colleges and universities. Jesuit influence in the early years, however, was felt through the faculty of St. Francis Seminary, Milwaukee, whose professors were largely alumni of the Jesuit University of Innsbruck. In the twentieth century, both before and after Vatican II, many of the Jesuits who were prominent in the renewal—such as John McKenzie, David Stanley, Joseph Fitzmyer, Richard McCormick and Walter Burghardt—came from a seminary teaching background. Jesuits have been prominent too in the post-Vatican II development of seminary cluster schools in Boston and Berkeley. Others have also contributed. Benedictines at St. Meinrad, Indiana, and in Kansas and Missouri have added the monastic and liturgical presence; Eudists, Trappists and Redemptorists have also had a hand in educating diocesan clergy.

Mention has already been made of Vatican II's "Decree on the Ministry and Life of Priests." Its direction for the spiritual development of priests was both different and traditional. The experience of the past twenty years is also ambiguous. Seminary life has changed enormously. The great majority of future priests are still educated in the autonomous seminaries clustered primarily around archdioceses. Some clusters centering on ecumenical cooperation with non-Catholic seminaries and universities have been organized, but they cater mainly to religious communities. The university-based seminary has not really taken off. Along with some swapping of real estate has gone a rather thoroughgoing revision of rules, professional ministry approaches, and expectations. A large amount of energy has been spent on psychological counseling. However, as the research on seminarians suggests, students have not changed radically in their hope for the spiritual life of the priesthood. They still see themselves as principally involved in sacramental ministry, counseling and consoling, praying and representing the church. They still think their first responsibility is to be holy.

Seminary programs are more consciously shaped around formation teams nowadays, so that there is an even greater emphasis on the awareness of the need for spiritual life. As always, it is difficult to determine how well-integrated these programs are with the lived experience, and especially with the academic experience, of the students. The recent "Letter of the Prefect of the Sacred Congregation for Catholic Education," following the visitation of American seminaries, rated them "generally satisfactory" from a Roman viewpoint.[8] "We have commended the sense of priestly purpose of most of the theologates and the attention they give to a balanced formation in the spiritual/liturgical, academic and pastoral dimensions." However, the first concerns voiced were that seminaries develop a clearer concept of the ordained priesthood and that they avoid a fragmentation of the enterprise by trying to educate too many different kinds of ministers. Obviously, the distinctiveness of priestly spirituality is even now a concern to the Congregation.

VINCENT DE PAUL (1581–1660 A.D.)

The two men had just arrived at the somewhat shabby door of a decaying building that seemed in danger of collapsing.

"Home again," said the younger as he put down a battered portmanteau.

"Home and without much to show for it, Antoine," said the older as he pulled from his pocket the key he had retrieved from the neighbors. He was a short man but solidly built, a peasant somewhat out of place in Paris, and yet he seemed to fit. Everything about him bespoke quickness. He spoke concisely, his hands and face ever part of his speech. Most striking of all though, his eyes seemed constantly alert, noticing all that went on around him with a somewhat bemused expression. He was evidently in charge. There was an air of enthusiasm about everything he did, and even when his most biting evaluations were given, there seemed to be a ring of optimism behind them.

"I thought it went rather well, Monsieur Vincent," the younger man replied. "We had three months and we did get things back in order at Maison-de-champs."

"Yes, and now that Monsieur Gradot, our good abbé, is back, they will begin to go to pieces again. Let us hope that he is still sober and that he doesn't start selling wine in the rectory as before." He pushed open the door and breathed the stale air. "Not a bad man," he went on. "Actually, better than most. But his family expected too much when he was given that parish. And him without any education to speak of. It's a wonder that he still had the ambition and the ability to say Mass for the people and to do some preaching. Except that they didn't believe him. How can you enter the pulpit to teach others when you have never practiced your teachings yourself?"

"I thought we did well," said Antoine Portail, his young companion. "We cleaned up the church and we emptied the tabernacle of all that money and all those papers he kept there."

"Don't forget the candles," chuckled Vincent. "And we did teach him to use the formula of absolution instead of the Hail Mary for confession."

"The people appreciated what we did," Portail said somewhat defensively.

"That they did," agreed Vincent. "They always do. But it won't work."

He stepped back from the building to study it. He seemed to size it up carefully, ignoring the parts that were in disrepair and concentrating on the size and bulk of it. "Here is where we must start," he said.

"This is where we live," said Portail. "What do you mean, start?"

"Start a seminary," replied Vincent. "Start with what the name tells us: Bons Enfants. We start with young boys, and we train them for years to become the kind of priests that France needs. That's what the Council of Trent advised, and that's what somebody will need to do." He seemed almost to be musing to himself.

"It won't work," Portail responded. "Charles Borromeo tried it a century ago and it still hasn't worked. Olier and your friend Francis de Sales tried it. Didn't Francis say that he gave up after he produced one good priest and had no hope of ever making another?"

"Well," said Vincent, "one good priest ought to be enough. And besides, just because it didn't work then is no reason to say it won't work now. No, Antoine, there is no work more important or higher in God's eyes than educating good priests. Here we will start, and the good God being willing, we shall see what happens."

The place was Paris, 1625. The "college" of the Bons Enfants was a tumbledown institution given to Vincent de Paul as
headquarters for a new group he and Monsieur Portail and a
few others had begun, calling it "The Congregation of the Mission." The "mission" they had in mind when they started was
not to send men to foreign countries, but to restore dignity and
spiritual value to the Catholic religion, especially among the
rural poor. While de Berulle sat in his oratory and contemplated
the Eternal High Priest forever redeeming the world, Vincent
wanted to go out on the streets and see it put to work.

However, in the years that followed and as he became one
of the best-known and most influential men in Paris, he shrewdly
learned about the political forces at work. The Concordat of
1516 had given the king of France the right to nominate men
for the important ecclesiastical offices in France. In effect, the
king received an ecclesiastical pork barrel. There was often
more money and prestige in these church offices than in political
appointments. They tended to be passed on by the nobility as
a title to power and patrimony within the Court. The de Gondis
controlled the Archbishopric of Paris for a hundred and nine
years. And some of the de Gondis were among the best of the
French nobility. Men were ordained priests simply as a business
proposition. Although Vincent de Paul was a Gascon peasant,
he knew something from personal experience about how the
system worked. His father had destined him as a bright young
son not to become a shepherd, but to become a priest and secure
a paying benefice that would help the whole family. Vincent
was ordained when he was about nineteen years old and already
had his eyes fixed on a modestly profitable position. However,
he had more ability than he thought and rose more rapidly than
fit the plan. Soon he was in Rome and Paris; he knew cardinals
and bishops, and noblemen and their ladies. And slowly in the
climbing years, he threw it all over. He came to realize it was
too little.

When he arrived in Paris, he found a remarkable group of

men: Cardinal de Berulle, de Condren, Jean-Jacques Olier, later John Eudes and the hatchet man, Adrian Bourdoise. All of them perceived that the political situation, with its "religious" wars, was bad enough but that the state of the church was even worse. Bourdoise summed it up by saying that "most of the priests live with their arms folded." Vincent was milder, although he said, "The church has no worse enemies than priests." Bourdoise called him a "wet hen" for not having the courage to say more. Once Vincent remarked that the Lord had promised that the church would endure to the end of time, but he didn't say that it would do so in France.

Mainly it was a question of money. The church was big business and the church was part of the government. How well the church was doing was most often measured by how well it could keep the people in line and deliver the goods. A priest's success was measured by how much revenue he had, how glittering was his train of followers, how luxurious his abode and how many titles he possessed.

The trouble started at the top with the appointments to bishoprics and abbeys and other such lucrative and influential positions. By the favor of the Queen Marguerite, Vincent was appointed to the Council of Conscience, the government commission that recommended appointments. For nearly ten years he tried to get good men into office. However, he had incurred the displeasure of Cardinal Mazarin, the prime minister, who was jealous of Vincent's influence with the queen, and eventually he was sacked. But by that time, he had a foot in another door.

He and his friends were convinced that they had to start at the bottom with future clergymen. So they tried to revive the idea of seminaries, as the Council of Trent had decreed. Before Mazarin, Cardinal Richelieu had had his good moments, when he supported Vincent. The key was to make priesthood a respectable and dignified vocation in its own right. Vincent said that if the Son of God had spent most of his time on earth training disciples, that was good enough for anyone. The simple thought of the Son of God who was a priest was the core idea. It was an ancient and not-too-subtle conviction, and Vincent among them was the least inclined to be theoretical about it. He saw one thing: The sheep were immensely precious because they resembled Jesus Christ. That was difficult enough to see. The shepherds had to be convinced of their own dignity; that was the only thing worthwhile in the priesthood. The endless clawing for dignities, revenues and social betterment simply had to stop. It was not going to be halted in mid-course. It was clear to all of them that a new generation of priests had to be raised up first. They went about it each in his own way. Vincent succeeded better than most because he was the most practical in trying and failing and trying again. Among his many endeavors was an attempt to rescue a fairly large contingent of deported Irish priests in Paris, most of whom were drunks. He didn't succeed, but that didn't keep him from trying.

Vincent was an odd bundle of contradictions. He was an extraordinary innovator but a dogged pursuer of objectives. Toward the end of his long life, he found the members of his own community losing interest in the seemingly endless hard work to which he had set them. He said to them one evening (December 6, 1658):

> Someone in the company might say, "Sir, I am in this world to preach the Gospel to the poor and you want me to work in seminaries; I wish to be free to do what I came here to do, namely, to give missions in the country and not to shut myself up in a town for the service of ecclesiastics." It would be an illusion, a great illusion, for a man not to be willing to train good priests, all the more so as there is nothing greater than a priest, to whom is given all power over the natural and mystical Body of Christ, the power to forgive sins. . . . I am mentioning these difficulties to you, my brothers, before they arise, because it may be that they will arise. I shall not be able to work much longer; I shall soon be passing hence; my age, my infirmities and the abominations of my life will not suffer God to allow me to remain longer on this earth. After my death, then, there may come men

with a spirit of opposition, and lazy men who will say, "Why bother ourselves with looking after these hospitals? How can we help so many people ruined by the wars and go on visiting them in their lodgings?" But what sort of men will they be who will strive to turn us away from those good works we have begun? They will be free-thinkers, free-thinkers, who ask after nothing but pleasure and amusement; who, provided they have a good dinner, do not trouble their heads about anything else. Who besides? They will be . . . it is better I should not say it. They will be men who coddle themselves (as he said this, he placed his hands under his armpits), men who have only a narrow outlook, who confine their views and designs to a fixed circumference within which they shut themselves up as in a point; they are unwilling to leave it, and if they are shown something outside of it and draw near to consider it, at once they withdraw to their center, like snails into their shells.

Vincent was the humblest of men and yet he never sacrificed his dignity or his honest views to anyone. He was accommodating and yet he was one of the most independent-minded men who ever lived.

The experiment with the Bons Enfants did not work too well either. After ten years, in 1636, he had twenty-two young men there but considered that only three or four of them were suitable for further training. However, by that time he was already off on another tack. He gave a twenty-day "retreat" for ordinands in Beauvais in 1628. He found that he really had to make it a training session, and it went over fairly well. He continued to develop the idea and to lengthen the training period. The concept spread to Paris, and then to many other French dioceses. Vincent had hit upon a formula that was beginning to work, and he had the men to do the job. In 1642, Richelieu underwrote the establishment of the first permanent "major" seminary in his diocese of Lucon. It had a course of one or two years and took in young men between the ages of twenty and twenty-five. The emphasis was on learning the disciplines of a holy life and the practical administration of sacraments and preaching. Vincent never gave up his idea of a school for young boys either, and so developed the formula for "minor" and "major" seminaries. By the time he died in 1660, he had established seminaries in France, Poland and Italy. He never boasted about this; to do so would have been a capital sin in his eyes. Yet on the other hand, he never denigrated his own dignity as a priest. He knew what he believed in and he was not to be easily shaken.

Bibliography

The standard biography of St. Vincent de Paul is by Pierre Coste, *The Life and Works of Saint Vincent de Paul* (Westminster, Md.: Newman, 1952), 3 vols. The Conferences are published in Pierre Coste, *Conferences of Saint Vincent de Paul,* translated by Joseph Leonard (Philadelphia: Eastern Province, 1963). Henri Daniel-Rops has written a delightful appreciation entitled *Monsieur Vincent* (New York: Hawthorne, 1961). A very important essay for our purposes is: Jacques Delarue, *The Missionary Ideal of the Priesthood* (privately published by the Vincentian Fathers).

REFLECTIONS

Vincent de Paul added nothing new or essential to the theological concept of priesthood. He scarcely used the word "character," and he certainly eschewed all analysis of it as obediential potency. But he did use the word "instrument" frequently, and he turned the usual meaning on its head. A priest was *only* an instrument of Jesus Christ, but he was that completely; he was not an instrument of the government, civil or ecclesiastical, nor of his family. Priests had been the cause of most of the trouble; now they had to show people how to see the divine within themselves, and most of all, they had to love people as they were.

He wrote no *Summa*; all of his writings were ad hoc letters or conferences. He never wrote a book or a treatise or anything else except organizational rules for his associates, clerical and lay. What he did, and did superbly, was to put his finger on the key to the current problems that came his way, to find a practical means of dealing with them and then to slug it out with patience. He was a shrewd and plodding man who specialized in "know-how," not in theories. He was university-educated himself, and he knew how to consult experts. Most of the important clerics with whom he dealt were of the upper class and had been educated in universities; the lower clergy seem to have had very little formal education and often were not even able to read Latin, their official language.

The situation was the inheritance of the medieval universities. During those past ages, the clergy had dominated the universities. Theology had become a "pure science." It had also become the access to influence in business and politics. That was largely the trigger for the Reformation: the corruption of a greedy priesthood. The Council of Trent in 1563 had recognized that and had decreed that the education of the clergy should return to the ancient concept of training "in the bishop's house." It was the most important decision of Trent, but nobody had found a way to implement it very well.

Vincent and the extraordinary men of his time tried. University education for the clergy certainly had its value, but it tended to neglect the very center of priestly being, namely, sanctity. One could become knowledgeable in arcane truths or heresies by attending universities; one could not lead a people to salvation by such an education. Vincent and Olier and John Eudes were convinced that priests must be given a specific education. It must be practical, drawn from parochial experience, but also solidly theological. Each of them tried to make such a system work; Vincent was the most successful.

He had clear ideas about what a priestly vocation was. He wrote to one of his priests about the "mission" of the congregation:

God has called us from all eternity and destined us to be missionaries; he neither called us to be born a hundred years before nor a hundred years after, but precisely at the time of the institution of this career. Hence, we should not see nor hope for any rest, satisfaction or blessing elsewhere than in the Congregation of the Mission, since it is there alone that God wishes and desires us to be, presuming of course that our vocation is a true one and not based on self-interest or the wish to free ourselves from the anxieties of life or any other human consideration.[9]

Vincent respected the personal choice that priesthood entailed, but he also repeated the classic understanding that a vocation comes directly from God:

Sir, we should keep for ourselves such liberty of choice that will be above all human considerations: "You have not chosen Me," said our Lord, "but I have chosen and destined you," so that we may know that He alone has the right to make a call to the work of the Gospel. That is the reason why there is a difference between one vocation and another as there is between the sun and the moon, and between day and night, because that which does not come from God is but a shadow of a real vocation, although it may be clothed in fine pretexts and in the same dress.[10]

Vincent also had a clear idea of what running a seminary entailed.

One of the things most required in the seminaries, as our experience shows, is that they have persons of interior life and great piety in order to inspire this spirit in the seminarians . . . ; The chief thing is to train clerics to devotion. And for that, Sir, we should be filled with it first, for it would be almost useless to give them instruction in it and no example.[11]

It was not greatly different from the advice he gave others. His letters to the Daughters of Charity, to the Ladies of Charity, to his various lay organizations and to members of the nobility and of the royalty were full of the same sentiments. But he was a man who singularly kept first things first, and he knew that good priests were the very first concern of the church. Fine theories would not suffice; a life lived in complete dependence on God was needed.

Vincent de Paul, along with King Louis IX and Joan of Arc, is a national hero of France. Voltaire had not much use for religion but confessed that Vincent de Paul was "my kind of saint." However, Vincent was a national hero for reasons other than for his work with priests. The man accomplished marvels in feeding the population of whole provinces during the religious wars; he laid the foundations for charitable organizations of all sorts; he applied solid common sense to getting the rich to help the poor in ways that they could do it best and to getting the poor to recognize their dignity as human beings. One of the lesser-known things about Vincent was his work with the "deserving poor," the nobility of Lorraine. The religious wars had left them without anything. Vincent organized a discreet "old boys' network" of his noble friends, which quietly took care of these supposedly undeserving rich.

His real importance for our consideration, however, and perhaps for his overall importance in church history, was his restoration of the priesthood to a dignified and independent position in society. Vincent never succeeded in abolishing the Concordat, which was the cause of so much trouble; he did his best to get ecclesiastical business out of politics. But then he turned to grass-roots education. He gave priests an honest pride in their own status, independent of money or titles. And he left the church a working model of how to educate new generations of priests.

4. The Vincentian Ideal of the Priest

The Vincentian ideal of the priest reached the United States in a somewhat fractured form. The community had been harshly treated by the French revolutionaries and restored by the French monarchy. The dominant French members and, through them the Irish, were hardly friends of freedom and personal liberty. Much of the nineteenth century community literature was bitterly anti-liberal. Add to this a touch of Jansenism, which the Founder had always feared and warned against, and the American version of Vincentianism emerged as somewhat puritanical and rigid. Nonetheless it survived and flourished, especially on the frontier, which is where the first seminary was established, at Perryville, Missouri.

Today there is a revival of interest in the authentic spirit of Vincent de Paul.[12] To Americans, Vincent has always been a model of practicality. He cannot be accused of promoting clerical privilege or elitism; he was too involved with engaging all classes of Catholics in social works. His picture of priests came somewhat from Berulle, but most of it came from his own broad experience in dealing with secular priests. Although he founded a community of priests, he always spoke to his confreres primarily as priests, not as religious (which they were not in the canonical sense). It is the priesthood that is his ideal. Unlike Berulle, and to a certain extent Olier, his emphasis was not directly on the holy God, but on people as a way to God.

Vincent stressed that a priest must totally forget himself and his achievements. For example, he wrote to one of his priests, Jacques Pesnelle: "I can only thank God for all the graces He has given you. You should humble yourself a lot in view of the effects of His divine goodness in you and through you, and because of the impediments you may be putting to the operation of His grace, which otherwise would produce still greater good. Be very careful, Sir, not to attribute any of it to yourself; you would commit theft and you would insult God, who alone is the author of all good things."[13]

By "redemptive work" Vincent had in mind the actual happenings he saw. He looked at the poor country people and he could say quite honestly that they seemed more like animals than like human beings. Then he said that priests had to see Jesus Christ in them. He had seen great good come from this, not because it was a clever technique, but because God stepped in. He had seen mothers abandon children and he had organized a group of lay helpers to meet that situation; he saw conditions improve. He had seen noblemen abandon the peer dictates of dueling when confronted with the example of Jesus. He had seen rich women become conscious of their Christian obligation to help the poor with their abundant wealth.

Especially he had seen priests survive failure only to become better priests. He had a great mistrust of clever ways, and particularly of clever success. One of his priests reported with great enthusiasm that he had obtained the backing of Cardinal Durazzo in Genoa against opponents, for which he expected a pat on the back. Vincent wrote:

> Yes, yes, we shall pray God for you and for those persons who are so fierce for revenge, and we shall have Masses said for that. Mine, if possible, will be celebrated at Notre Dame according to your intention; but after all, will you not agree that our care and our prayers will be ineffectual, if such is God's good pleasure? For, Sir, what would happen if everything was a success for us, and what right have we, poor creatures as we are, to claim success always? We have less to worry about when someone resists our weak persuasion. Since God is satisfied with our good will and our true efforts, let us also be content with the results He gives them and our actions will never be without return. I tell you all this on account of the displeasure you feel that some are not benefitting by your missions; for you must not be surprised; but rather, Sir, let us judge that everything is going at the world's best when we are not satisfied with it, provided that we know how to humble ourseves and to redouble our confidence in God.[14]

Human weaknesses never seemed to discourage Vincent, whether his own or those of others. He wrote to one of his priests: "You have great reason to distrust yourself, but you have greater reason to trust in Him. If you have an inclination to evil, you know that He has an incomparably greater one to do good, and to do it even in you and through you."[15]

He insisted most of all that priests should be completely dependent on God, both in initiating action and in evaluating the consequences. God dominated in all. Vincent was very practical about this. He never wanted to be in competition with other religious groups; he never wanted to push his own pet ideas; he never wanted to be hasty. "I see nothing more common than the ill success of affairs that have been rushed," he wrote.[16] God would get things done as he wanted in good time.

Vincent saw an incredible amount accomplished in his lifetime. He was not afraid to take chances and to fail; he simply tried another way. Although he was remembered especially for his social projects in helping the poor during times of war and depression, he had relatively few theories about this work. He simply asked what Jesus Christ would do in any concrete situation. And he believed in hard work. His saying, "Let us love God, my brothers, but let it be with the strength of our arms and the sweat of our brows," became a Vincentian slogan.

Of all people, Vincent best exemplifies the tension that contemporary theologians speak of as existing between charism and office, between function and the something that distinguishes priests. To priests he insisted on the immense dignity God had conferred on them by ordination, the dignity of doing the same things that Jesus Christ did. He did remind them of the specific priestly duties of saying Mass well, of being always ready to administer the sacraments (although very little is said about this in his own life), and especially of catechizing well. Vincent was insistent that preaching be instructive; he was a fierce opponent of bombastic or merely emotional sermons. He wanted to get the message across, and he wanted it to have solid food in it. He took the same attitude toward formation of the clergy: spiritual formation, yes, but based on sound education. That was Vincent's way.

5. Going My Way?

The Vincentian vision of priestly spirituality fits into the American scene today. It is only one among others of such ideals. However, it has unique qualities that equip it for present necessities. It needs to be reinterpreted, and especially it needs to be lived.

The education of the American clergy has been largely practical. Instead of dwelling on "hi-tech" theological research, most of us who teach in seminaries have aimed at giving solid, overall instruction to the general practitioners among the clergy. The aim has fitted comfortably with the Vincentian approach. Vincentians and others have often been criticized for being "anti-intellectual." Vincent de Paul occasionally chided well-educated priests who made a display of their learning. But he also knew, as a degreed man himself, the importance of education. He said: "Although all priests are bound to be learned, we are none the less specially obliged to it because of the employments which the Providence of God has called us to, such as the work for the ordinands, the direction of seminaries and missions, even though experience shows that those who speak most familiarly and most popularly succeed the best. . . . Still, we must have knowledge."[17] He more often rebuked those practical men who had clever plans for success. If Vincent was practical, it was with a practicality that understood how the church really worked, namely, God accomplished what he wanted to. We had to stand back and let him do it.

So also Vincentian seminary formation was not aimed at simple pragmatism in the sense of training men for functional jobs. In fact, "practical" instruction in the sense of "hands-on" training was never a high priority. Vincent admired Bourdoise, who set up a practical seminary at the parish church of St. Nicholas de Chardonnet in Paris, but he never tried to imitate him. Perhaps he foresaw what actually happened: Parish seminaries of that sort were taken over by bishops. The Vincentian system was not opposed to the "practical" and always carried some touch of it, but neither was it specifically geared to it. "Practical" meant not only sound academic traning, but—and especially—spiritual formation. The practical part was the desire to teach young men that success was not a necessary ingredient of the good priestly life. Zeal was, but what happened after that had to be seen and accepted as what God wanted. This was the most "practical" goal of Vincentian education, and it would have been no matter whether the objective had been to train scholars or brick-and-mortar priests.

We say today that materialism and success are our besetting sins, but we do not do much to make the struggle with these sins a lived reality. We go on acting as though better management or better resources or better social action could remedy the evil. Certainly we must have professionalism in the church, but we must always be willing to admit the limitations of human means, even when of the finest.

We need people who can see behind the facade to the spiritual realities involved. Vincent de Paul put great stress on the Incarnation, not as a theological thesis, but as a very practical way of seeing Christ in every human being and in every human event. That is where the mystery factor enters. That is what the world needs today. Our people have the intelligence and the expertise to work out the problems; so too do our priests. What we need is a "seer." We have enough "prophets," especially prophets of doom, in our political, social and environmental arenas. We need wise men who can discern the real world of the spirit behind the confusing parade of life's events. If a priest's efforts meet with success, he must have the spiritual vision to see that success as a work of God. If his efforts fail, he must see that also as a work of God, leading him on to something more.

Humility and obedience are dignified human responses to the mysteries of the spiritual world around us. That is what we must recognize, and that is what the American church must acknowledge today. We need not fear that the generality of Americans will be passive or lazy; we simply are not made that way. We need to challenge all, not only Catholics, to broaden their vision to include the spiritual realities and to walk with us. On the other hand, we would do better if we openly admitted that a power struggle is going on within the church. Perhaps it is inevitable; like the poor, it is always with us. But it is too easy to lose sight of humility and obedience when faced with the polarity of a tug-of-war.

The Vincentian seminary training tried to discern the dignity of each human being. In seminaries this often amounted to "tough love." It was not the custom to applaud and grant many certificates of achievement. There are no heroes in seminaries, neither among faculty nor students. It was the custom to take people seriously, to deal with them as adults and challenge them to achieve. Love and dignity went together, and each was demanding. As with most things human, such ideals were not always attainable, they didn't always work, and students years later would remember the excesses. But the seminaries also had a curious habit of acting on what did work. It is certainly not a giant step to see in this day, when Catholics are often identified by their championship of "Respect Life," that such an attitude in the training of priests is an essential ingredient.

Vincent de Paul was the least elitist of men. Oddly enough, he had much to say to his priests about the dignity and responsibility of the priestly calling, as though it were totally distinctive, and yet he could apply the very same spiritual lessons to the great number of lay people whom he inspired and organized. Today we are trying to create a practical way by which all ministers in the church may work together. Vincent found a way to do it years ago. Vincentians have always had other people associated with them: Daughters of Charity, Ladies of Charity, even St. Vincent de Paul Societies, which were started much later by Frederick Ozanam. These relationships should be updated, not simply continued as previously. Nonetheless, this is part of the charism of the organization and a much-needed one in the church today.

Vincentians teaching in diocesan seminaries have always been proud that they were legally as well as in spirit a part of the diocesan clergy. It is no mere boast. The spirituality of diocesan priests need be no different than that which Vincent taught. That spirituality is based on the conviction that although the recipient of Orders is distinct by reason of office, he, like all the baptized, is simply an instrument in the hands of God. Vincent was very specific about what he meant by this. He meant that priests should accept as the will of God every job they are assigned. We need, of course, to understand that vision in the present operating procedures involving consultation. But a diocese or a religious community is not an employment agency trying to find the kind of job each individual desires. Nor is the local priest a free agent, able to create the kind of church or community that he wants. God has willed priests to be part of a presbyterate. Obedience is still an essential part of the mission. Certainly, on the example of Vincent, this does not eliminate initiative; he was one of the most innovative of men. But it must involve a mature discernment of the Spirit in order to let God do the leading and the achieving. Too often "discernment" has turned out to be an unassailable justification for what we wanted to do. American seminary education needs the Vincentian and Sulpician vision today. The breadth and depth of that tradition can temper the temptation to overprofessionalize the education of contemporary American priests.

SIX

The Non-distinctiveness of the Catholic Priest

1. Introduction

"You, however, are a chosen race, a royal priesthood, a holy nation, a people he claims for his own to proclaim the glorious works of the One who called you from darkness into his marvelous light" (1 Peter 2:9). This text is often cited to illustrate the priestly ministry of all the baptized, sometimes in contrast to the approach that says the Catholic priest is distinct by reason of priestly ordination. It is worth investigating the biblical background to shed some light on the present way in which priests fit into the total mission of the church.

The key words are actually a quote from Exodus 19:6: "You shall be to me a kingdom of priests, a holy nation." Exodus 19 is a composite, or a redactor's composition, set as an introduction to the Sinaitic Covenant. As such, it represents the more mature theological reconsideration of an earlier insight. Moses first tells the chosen people that they must remember the past favors of God. The admonition is stated poetically rather than

151

historically: "You have seen for yourselves how I treated the Egyptians and how I bore you up on eagles' wings and brought you here to myself" (Exodus 19:4). The poetic metaphor of those eagles' wings must be noted. It is not a legal nor an administrative principle. Moses's people that are chosen to be a kingdom of priests, a holy nation, simply says that they were chosen primarily to worship God, that they do this by keeping themselves separate (holy) in following their distinctive Way of the Lord. Immediately following are instructions on how they are to sanctify themselves for receiving the Covenant at the mountain.

No one in Judaism ever saw a contradiction between the nation as a "kingdom of priests" and the very institutional priesthood. Priests were of hereditary lineage in the tribe of Aaron, although the history of this custom is checkered. They were primarily cultic persons commissioned to serve in precise ways in the temple. Less clearly, they were also designated as "teachers" of the law, apparently catechists of the basic doctrine. One theory has it that the "Priestly Document in the Pentateuch "is actually a catechism for children. At any rate, the tradition claimed that "the lips of the priest are to keep knowledge, and instruction is to be sought from his mouth, because he is the messenger of the Lord of hosts" (Malachi 2:7). Thus Malachi denounced the priests of his time for failing in an essential duty.

The basic consciousness of being "chosen" continues into the New Testament. As Paul saw it, we did not become Christians because we were convinced by logical argument or because of our personal choice; we were chosen and had to respond. Neither was the choice made primarily for our own advantage; we were chosen to proclaim the saving work of Jesus Christ. "Holiness" entails the hard work of living virtuously and differently so that we may carry out this task. This is the train of thought in 1 Peter 2:9-10: "You are a chosen race, a royal priesthood, a holy nation, a people he claims for his own to proclaim the glorious works of the One who called you from darkness into his marvelous light. Once you were no people; but now you are God's people; once there was no mercy for you, but now you have found mercy." It is an early mission statement on evangelization.

The verses have nothing to do with cultic functions as such, nor is there any sign that they fit poorly with the structures of the Petrine church, whatever they may have been. Like Exodus 19:6, they do not constitute a legal or an administrative principle. Note has been taken earlier of the historical theology concerning the manner in which Christ first made himself known as a rabbi and teacher and, at the end, of how he commissioned all who would follow him to teach the Gospel. At the same time, he instructed a special group and set it apart. In the Synoptic Gospels, this special group becomes the recipient of most of his instruction. I Peter is an exhortation based on Exodus 19, touched up with additional images, designed to inspire Christians to live up to their high calling of holiness, not to counter the basic organizational structure.

In the second and third centuries of the Christian era, the imagery of the Old Testament priesthood began to be applied to the bishops, priests and deacons of the Christian communities, as the sacramentaries (such as given in the "Apostolic Tradition," circa 215 A.D.) attest. However, the trajectory should be noted. It was the imagery, not the structural details, that was applied. The Christian priesthood was never hereditary; it was never concentrated almost exclusively on cultic functions; it was not divorced from apostolic preaching and teaching. Instead, the emphasis was on the ancient concepts of "sacrifice" and "holiness."[1] The first concept would have been derived normally from the general usage of "priest"; the second was unique in stressing not ritual purity, but true personal holiness.

Then, from an apparently minor characteristic of the Old Testament priesthood, there developed the notion of priest/bishop as teacher. The concept was so strong in the New Testament that leadership in the first centuries, at least as much as we know of it from the written evidence, centered on teaching the authentic message of the Gospel and exploring the meanings behind it. The great Christological discussions among the Fathers and the divergent writings and preachings of heretics illustrate how much development of doctrine occurred. The structure of the Christian priesthood grew in a way that was independent of the priesthood of the Old Testament even while some of the imagery was preserved as a theological explanation of what priests actually did. The recently revised "Rite of Ordination" goes back to this Old Testament imagery.

2. Vatican II and the Common Priesthood

Vatican Council II was very conscious of reviving this ancient tradition of the common priesthood of all the faithful. The basic document on the church, entitled *Lumen Gentium*, stated:

> Christ is the great prophet who proclaimed the kingdom of the Father both by the testimony of his life and by the power of his word. Until the full manifestation of his glory, he fulfills this prophetic office, not only by the hierarchy who teach in his name and by his power, but also by the laity. He accordingly both establishes them as witnesses and provides them with the appreciation of the faith and the grace of the word so that the power of the Gospel may shine out in daily family and social life. They show themselves to be the children of the promise if, strong in faith and hope, they make the most of the present time and with patience await the future glory. Let them not hide this their hope then, in the depths of their hearts, but rather express it through the structure of their secular lives in continual conversion and in wrestling "against the world rulers of this darkness, against the spiritual forces of iniquity" (Ephesians 6:12).[2]

So also the "Decree on the Life and Ministry of Priests" begins by putting this ministerial priesthood into the context of the common priesthood:

The Lord Jesus "whom the Father consecrated and sent into the world" (John 10:36) makes his whole Mystical Body sharer in the anointing of the Spirit wherewith he has been anointed: for in that Body all the faithful are made a holy and kingly priesthood, they offer spiritual sacrifices to God through Jesus Christ, and they proclaim the virtues of him who has called them out of darkness into his admirable light. Therefore there is no such thing as a member that has not a share in the mission of the whole Body. Rather, every single member ought to reverence Jesus in his heart, and by the spirit of prophecy give testimony of Jesus.[3]

The Decree goes on to distinguish between the ministerial priesthood and the common priesthood. The 'Decree on the Apostolate of Lay People' has the same theme:

'Every activity of the Mystical Body with this in view goes by the name of "apostolate";' the Church exercises it through all its members, though in various ways. In fact, the Christian vocation is, of its nature, a vocation to the apostolate as well . . . In the Church there is diversity of ministry but unity of mission. To the apostles and their successors Christ has entrusted the office of teaching, sanctifying and governing in his name and by his power. But the laity are made to share in the priestly, prophetical and kingly office of Christ; they have therefore, in the Church and in the world, their own assignment in the mission of the whole People of God. In the concrete, their apostolate is exercised when they work at the evangelization and sanctification of men; it is exercised too when they endeavor to have the Gospel spirit permeate and improve the temporal order, going about it in a way that bears witness to Christ and helps forward the salvation of men. The characteristic of the lay state being a life led in the midst of the world and of secular affairs, laymen are called by God to make of their apostolate, through the vigor of their Christian spirit, a leaven in the world.[4]

The general theme of "priestly people" is still ringing clear in the foregoing. However, despite the Council's efforts to explain how the ministerial priesthood and the common priesthood complement one another, there is still ambiguity.

3. The Spheres

In the official texts there is a tendency to speak of a sphere for lay ministry and a sphere for priestly ministry. Talk of "spheres" is redolent of an earlier application to church and state in official documents. The attempt was made to define certain temporal concerns that were the legitimate sphere of action for the perfect society of the state; there were other spiritual areas in which the church operated as a perfect society. The state had no interest in the church canonizing another saint; the church could care less about the state raising or lowering the speed limit. We do not hear much of that talk recently. The concept never worked very well in practice. There was an overlapping that was admitted, but unfortunately it was precisely in the area of the overlapping of the spheres that the real problems lay. When today the government allocates money for abortions, talk of the two separate spheres is of little help.

Something similar seems to be happening when we divide the apostolate into that of the laity and that of the clergy. The idea sounds good at first, but then it seems to evaporate when we get to the really tough problems in the overlapping areas. Two problems connected with lay ministry seem to lend most to the confusion at present: education and placement.

The most intense efforts of the clergy to educate the laity have been made in theological education. Seminaries and universities have admitted lay students to degree programs that were formerly populated almost solely by priesthood candidates. We now have a fair number of lay Catholics who are educated on a par with priests. We probably have made sufficient provision for educating enough of these special people. They are special people for whom we have neither a distinctive name nor definition. We need to be aware of this since it forms a real problem.

In the two spheres theory which seems to prevail even today in official documents, the laity by and large should be educated in order to "permeate and improve the temporal order", to "express it through the structure of their secular lives". We ought to be educating laity to carry the message into advertising, education, sports, research, law, family care, and so forth. The laity should be educated to infiltrate the workaday world, not to do priests' work. What we need is adult education within professional and vocational groups that will study the implications of Christian living within their sphere. We also need Catholic universities that are truly Catholic. They, not seminaries, should be responsible for educating the laity.

However, one need only look at the placements offered these lay graduates from seminaries and theological departments. They are not placed back in "secular lives," or in the "temporal order." They get jobs in church organizations. Certainly such jobs are useful and there is no reason why priests should fill them all. The only point being made here is that up to the present, our educational and placement services have been putting our educated lay persons in the wrong positions—if we believe in educating the laity for their distinctive role.

A good amount of the tension comes from the fact that we have not yet been able to name or define these special people who function as coworkers with and for the clergy and the general members. They are professional church workers in a sense. In older times brothers and sisters filled this category. We did not have legal definitions for them either, but somehow we had a working agreement about where they fitted in. Sometimes it did not work for their full dignity; sometimes they managed to get a great share of authority. We just haven't developed a realistic understanding as yet of what the proper function of such persons is, whether they be religious or lay professionals. In the confusion, the laity has sometimes seemed to undermine the role of the clergy, and we fail to understand why we are angry on both sides.

4. The Priest and the Theologian

It is almost instinctive to think of all priests as theologians and all theologians as priests. However, the latter is obviously not true, especially today, and the former is only a somewhat thin courtesy. "Priest" and "theologian" are different species. The need for making a distinction has arisen recently in disputes over the academic freedom of theologians. The Catholic Theological Society of America made the following distinction in 1986:

> Can theology as a scholarly discipline simply function as a re-statement of official church teaching, or does it also have expository, creative and critically probing functions? Is the theologian's role primarily that of echoing the hierarchial magisterium, a chief qualification for which would be unquestioning adherence to the totality of present teaching? Or is the theologian's role the seeking of understanding in faith, especially in the light of the challenging questions of the day, the chief qualifications for which would be academic competency and communion with the church? The vast majority of our Society's membership opts for the second and more traditional of each of the above pairs.[5]

In brief, the Statement makes a distinction between the professional theologian, who is seeking understanding on the basis of academic competency, and the vocational priest or hierarch, who hands on the totality of present teaching. In effect, the professional theologians are not to be identified as "catechetical arms of the official church."[6] This seems perfectly clear.

But is it? We seem to be instinctively going back to another two-spheres theory. The Statement concerns the case of "Rev. Dr. Charles Curran." It is curious that both titles are used. Although "priest" and "theologian" can be separated in theory and easily enough when the theologian is a lay person, when one is both, it is difficult to do so in practice. "Priest" and "dry-fly fisherman" can certainly be separated. But can the ordinary priest in the pulpit be confined to simply "handing on the totality of present teaching?" As the living interpreter of the Gospel, he too must "seek understanding, especially in the light of the challenging questions of the day." Even in the most academic situation, it is diffcult for "Dr. Curran" or any of us to dissociate ourselves completely from the "Rev."

The attempt to find an historical justification for this complete separation is probably as futile as seeking the "historical Jesus."[7] The same may be said of lay theologians. If there is a point at which the common priesthood of all the baptized comes into play, undoubtedly it is in the area in which defining the god to be worshiped is under question. The lay theologian also has an obligation to be "in communion with the church," as the Statement says. This is not a restriction of academic freedom; it is an admonition that scientific theology does not have all the answers.

We are certainly enriched and instructed in theological inquiry today by the research and writing of lay theologians. Presumably they are in touch with the practical problems of the lay apostolate, especially in such non-clerical areas as family life as it is actually lived. We need to listen to them. As a matter of fact, we need to listen to those among them who are not professional theologians. If the apostolate of all the baptized is to be lived in the secular world, we need to know about that secular world in practical terms. As Andrew Greeley has remarked, theological problems are not to be solved by taking polls.[8] Neither are they to be solved by ignoring the de facto situation among the laity.

5. The Common Priesthood in the American Church

The current "in word" is that the clergy must empower the laity for the evangelization of the world. It makes for inspiring reading but it has little to do with common sense or facts. "Empower" is a patronizing word; it intimates that "power brokers" can effectively transfer power to others. There is no reason in theology or in history to think that this is true. Of course it will be objected that this is not what is intended. However, it is what happens too frequently. A lay person who wants to work in a special apostolate must first obtain professional training. Then he or she must look for a job, probably for one in a parish or a diocesan office. If successful, such a person may rise in position to having an office and a secretary at the Catholic Center. The person is now "empowered," i.e., he or she has power in an office the clergy has provided and a working budget the clergy will approve. The power is in the job.

The most visible signs of the shift in power have been those of the transfer of action from the customary cultic duties of priests to the laity. The movement of priests into the secular affairs of the laity is almost invisible—except in an odd way. By the first I mean that priests have not become workers on the model of the French Worker Priest movement of the fifties; nor have they become businessmen; nor have they offered to become surrogate parents on any notable scale. Priests have not moved into the secular sphere of the laity about which the Council spoke; the laity have moved into the cultic and teaching and counseling sphere of the clergy. On the other hand, there has been an odd movement of priests into professional spheres.

One need only look at the Official Catholic Directory to be impressed by the great number of activities that now fall directly under the diocesan chancery offices.[9] There are Catholic Charities that cover many bureaus, offices, directors and so forth, for housing, social works, reeducation, counseling services, senior citizens' centers, youth centers, to mention a few. Much of this activity is involved with government. There are cemetery associations with large amounts of real estate and other financial assets; there are insurance offices, building commissions, planning departments, personnel-placement bureaus. Usually there is a priest at the head of these activities. He may be only one priest amidst a numerous staff, but he has had to get into the professional business of running the office and he probably has had professional training of an academic nature.

This is repeated analogously at the parish level. For example, someone will suggest that the parish should have a senior citizens' center, a drug and-alcoholism counseling service, a service for the divorced and widowed, a social-concerns department, an organization for the poor, a planning committee for buildings. All of these undertakings are, of course, admirable. And it is up to Father to organize them. In the course of this, he is expected to learn at least something of the formal structures and procedures of such fields. Eventually, if they become large enough, specially trained priests are expected to head them up. In an odd way, the clergy are moving into these non-priestly professions, and they often find them very congenial. Where have all the priests gone? A lot of them have disappeared into chancery offices or professional jobs.

Meanwhile, a good number of truly lay organizations, often ethnic in origin, have decreased in numbers and importance.[10] We have a few lay publications, not many. There were formerly many more. The Centralvereins, the Polish Athletic Clubs, the Catholic Workers, the Daily Catholic, the St. Vincent de Paul Societies, the Legion of Mary—in effect, the more or less independent lay organizations have either been absorbed by the chancery office or have gone out of business. As noted earlier, the realistic model of the Catholic Church in the United States is the corporation, and it is becoming a multidiocesan corporation—and will probably become multinational. We already know the dangers involved in this bureaucratic model by the one already existing in Rome.

6. The Problem of How to Do It

We talk confidently about the laity taking their rightful place in the church as ministers. And we know that there is a change going on at the grass-roots level. But the change is not really very great. The percentage of Catholics who attend Mass regularly has not noticeably increased; in fact, it has declined slightly since Vatican II.[11] There has been a considerable increase in the number of people who receive the Eucharist and we do not know why. There has been a noticeable drop in the number and frequency of confessions, and we do not know why. The Gallup poll indicates that of late there is a general increase of interest in religion in America, but that interest has not shown up notably in the number of social programs, except perhaps spottily among some fundamentalist sects.

We should be somewhat guarded in talking enthusiastically about the increased role of the laity in the ministry of evangelization. Any pastor can probably recite by rote the rule that one third of the people always contribute generously, one third parsimoniously, and one third not at all. This rule of thumb is probably somewhat applicable to other activities of the Catholic community. It has not changed much over the years. Those who are enthusiastic for becoming real ministers in the common priesthood are better-educated professionally today and more upwardly mobile in the society of the church. They would probably have been active church members at any time.

Before we make too many blanket statements, we should look at the real situation. Some members of the church are showing great enthusiasm and zeal for ministerial work that sometimes cuts across functions formerly expected of priests. Some Catholics want to narrow the gap between the clergy and the laity. Some Catholics want a larger voice in decision-making. And some think that "that is what priests are for and let's leave it to them." Polls showing that such and such a percentage favor married priests, or women priests, or community parishes that select their own leaders, should be looked upon with some suspicion. It is easy for those who have little stake in the matter and no intention of making any great sacrifices to favor proposals that seem to be popular or avant-garde. As with political prediction, we do not know what people really believe until they go to the polls and lay their convictions on the line.

This brings us to the problem of how we expect the church to operate. It is understandable that when the Fathers of Vatican II in Rome popularized the expressions "collegiality" and "subsidiarity," we in America translated them into "democratic procedures." We know that that is wrong and we make a knee-jerk rejection of it. But that does not change our feelings as an American society. We do expect to be consulted; it is our money. We do expect our opinion to be valued; it is one man, one vote. We do expect equality; it is in our Constitution as law of the land and custom. We have not worked out these matters. We have had bishops dialoguing with many people before they issue a pastoral letter on peace or economics. There is still a large residue of Catholic opinion that asks, "What do they know about it?" or, "Why weren't we consulted?" The entrance of the laity into the older preserve of the priest has been relatively easy compared to the entrance of the priest into the realm of the laity.

We have not been able to develop a really viable procedure for the laity to carry out that distinctive role of evangelization in the secular world that the Council spoke of, nor for the clergy to exercise leadership in encouraging the people to do so. We are on our way and we may well be pleased with what has happened thus far. But we should not deceive ourselves into thinking we have cracked the code of proper procedure in this matter. The problem of the distinctiveness of the laity is at least as difficult as the problem of the nondistinctiveness of the clergy. The strength to be had from a committed core of men, even if operating poorly, is so clear that it need not be argued. To think that the laity will en masse rise up and take over all the work of the church is simply unrealistic.

SEVEN

Journey Into The Unknown

1. Where Is God?

In ancient times the high priest went into the Holy of Holies once a year. It was his most sublime duty. He and he alone could enter. In the time of Christ, the Holy of Holies was an absolutely empty room; the Ark of the Covenant had been lost. The final act of the high priest was to visit an empty room. The culmination of the Christian story was an empty tomb.

Now the suggestion of applying this kind of high-priestly imagery to a Catholic priest will be very inspiring to some, as it has been during the ages, and very offensive to others. Objection may be lodged to the high-priest image, which is unabashedly hierarchical. Or perhaps the very notion of one priest allowed this exclusive experience may grate on those who place first the equality of all the baptized. Perhaps the idea of a priest walking into a secret room instead of going out into the world to combat social injustice and work out his "preferential option

167

for the poor" is odious. And, of course, the priest is presumably masculine, which offends others.

All of these attitudes have something worthwhile to say and can point to something in the tradition to support them. It may be much or little, but it is there, and it is expressed today. Meanwhile, the individual priest must get on with the business of being a priest, and he must act out of an image. If he refuses to choose, he simply dissolves into a nonentity. If he chooses one over the other, he probably offends someone. He certainly has the right, as does any other Christian, to take a strong stand in favor of any of the views within the parameters of faith, and as a leader, he should do so.

Obviously we are dealing with images in conflict, no matter how many pages of erudite scholarship may try to define the right and the wrong. In practice, the individual priest probably acts at one time out of one image and at another time out of a different one. All human beings do that in diverse circumstances. Only institutions and bores even try to be consistent. NCR is insistently liberal and the Wanderer is unalterably conservative. In real life we do not value consistency as highly. The parent confronted with a domestic uprising by children hovers between the image of hugging the kids and slapping them down. The solution probably varies from incident to incident. That is the way most of our ethical decisions are made.[1] They are choices in faith amidst conflicting images.

It may be objected that we cannot inject personal images into theological discussion and reach an intellectually acceptable conclusion. There is truth in the objection. But in the practical world, very few theological arguments have ever been solved by being won. All those debates between the Reformers and Catholics should make that evident. Yet a decision about Christian living is still possible. Theological argumentation does not exhaust the ways in which we can reach suitable decisions. Let us at least essay an approach.

What is going on here? Where is God in this mess? Presumably where God has always been, right in the middle of it.

Such are the biblical stories about conflicting images and persons. The end is paradox, not solution. Now I am aware that we are quite reluctant to admit paradox as anything more than a literary gimmick that goes nowhere in our reasonable discussions. I would adduce that it is not so. Paradox exists first of all in the real world before we try to reduce it to literary trivia.

Most of the essential and operative truths of the faith are paradoxes. We believe firmly in one God: Father, Son and Holy Spirit. We believe in Jesus Christ: Son of God and Son of Mary. We believe that she was his mother and the mother of God, and we believe that the mother was a virgin. We believe that we are to be saved by faith in a gracious God—and that we must work out our salvation with fear and trembling. The literary formulations are almost always paradoxical. But before the literary expression existed, the reality existed and was itself a paradox. Even theology would not be a very exciting pursuit if that were not true. The answers could all be computerized.

Paradox is not a dead end but the discovery of a new dynamism that begins a whole new life of its own.[2] To cite an obvious example, all of us have some information about AA and its derivative programs in drugs, obesity, psychological trauma, and so forth. It is program that seems to be effective—not always, but more often than others. Yet intellectually it is a contradiction in terms. The very first step must be to admit that one is absolutely powerless over the debilitating factor before one can do anything about it. The victims are acutely aware of diametrically competing self-images; grandiosity and worthlessness, fear and a desire for security, disgust and exaltation. The paradox must be experienced at its utmost intensity, that of "hitting bottom," before a new dynamic of help from without is admitted.

Not only does this "work" ("happen" would be a better word), but it is perfectly Christian. Paul in Romans 7 describes himself in precisely such a situation. It is the keynote of that Epistle that the man who lives is justified by faith, not by works of the law. It does not matter to Paul or to our present experience which law is involved—the laws of logic, the laws of psychological development, the laws of management. One must first stand back far enough to acknowledge that there are combatants and then admit to powerlessness to control the situation. We are often afraid to do that; we have not hit bottom yet. But once the admission has been made, God must give grace. Only then is there empowerment to do something about the situation.

2. The Priestly Office

The picture in the Epistle to the Hebrews is that of Christ, a layman and the Son of God, going into that emptiness to make the final and unrepeatable sacrifice of himself as "one of his brothers" (Hebrews 2:17). The event is filled with paradox. In order to do it, he disappears from them; he goes to visit a God who is not there. Such paradoxes abound in New Testament ministry. If one is to save one's life, one must lose it for Christ's sake and the sake of the Gospel (Mark 8:35). In the last discourse in John, the twelve are told to be in the world but not of the world (John 17:9–19). Mystery is at the center of these practical instructions. These special men of Christ's are not functionaries who perform set rituals at specified times, as pagan priests were; they are men who summon the whole world to worship God, to see God in everything that happens in the universe, not only the evidently good but the apparently bad, and to lead believers on to a life that eye has not seen nor ear heard. Such was Augustine's thesis of the City of God, or if you will, making present the Kingdom of God.

Priests do this in a Christian community at a specific time and place, but it is really a cosmic event. God is made present in this place, but he is also made present for the whole world. The "other" and the "in" are constantly juxtaposed. All the baptized are called upon to have this spiritual insight and action, and probably in some way all human beings have been so called from the beginning. The priest is different by reason of an office, not by reason of a human sensitivity to such issues. The priest is an interpreter of faith by office. He does this first of all by presiding over the liturgies of a community as a representative of the whole presbyterate. Worship is and always has been a human activity full of symbolism and mystery. One must first get in touch with the invisible world of the spirit. It is a different kind of activity than people engage in during their normal working or recreational hours. It is awesome, dangerous and hidden. For this a priest has always been required. His presiding over the whole ritual, from beginning to end, is intended to ensure that it shall authentically reflect the faith of the community. It is he who arranges that the individuals present can partake of the larger and deeper faith they all share as a catholic community.

Any liturgy may be arranged for multiple purposes. It may be planned to be entertaining. Much magnificent music has been written for the Mass, and we make great attempts today to find suitable contemporary music and accompaniments to satisfy our needs and tastes. Obviously that is good as an enrichment of the liturgy. It may, however, become an interpretation of liturgy as a dramatic presentation primarily intended to please and to stir up good feelings. The decision as to the need the liturgy should serve is not left to the personal tastes of the priest. The presider must ensure that it interprets the faith of the community. It must interpret the drama of redemption that is taking place among the congregation; it must interpret the sacrifice of the whole community; and it must interpret the upward movement of the community in its praise of God and its prayer that help will come from above.

So also the liturgy of the Word within this redemptive drama must bring the meaning of the written record to the people. They already know the stories and the instructions; they already have the faith. The teacher must add to the set record the interpretation of its meaning in the daily life of today. That is what the Bible itself did for its contemporary readers; that is what he who has the office of instructor in the community must do. Together with the bishop and the presbyterate, he is the one who illuminates the minds of the baptized about the authentic Gospel and challenges the community to put it into action in its life; all who have the charism of teachers must do this. The priest is not the "answer man," as the seminarian sometimes pictures himself. Nor is he simply an individual giving a private interpretation. He may not be the most professionally competent to do this, but still, it is his job to interpret authentically in the light of the community's belief.

That belief must be "apostolic" in the sense that it is authentically in line with its origins; it is the priest's office as part of a presbyterate of a bishop to assure that it is. Perhaps the great importance given to the Apostles in New Testament literature and the extremely meager hints about priests is easily understood. The Apostles were the ones "sent" without limitation. In the beginning there was a whole wide world out there that needed to be told of the Good News; there were very few Christian communities that needed to be further catechized in the faith they already had. As the communities multiplied, the need for the teacher who taught within the community increased. As in Old Testament times, the priest became the one whose lips kept instruction. He was the teacher within the community; others were called upon to become the apostles, the missionaries. The cry today is for more priests to serve the community; evangelization has become a broader-based activity of the whole church.

So also has the priest by office the responsibility for reconciliation within the community. Obviously the Sacrament of Reconciliation falls under this unique function. But reconciliation is a community affair, not simply a one-to-one confession. As soon as the community is recognized as a community, it becomes an organization, and organizations always have divergences of opinion, usually unreconciled. In the circumstances of the American church today, endless programs flow from chancery offices to local parishes, and priests are called upon to put them into operation. These programs rarely meet with one hundred-percent acceptance, and there are always people who will take them over for their own private advantage. Conflict within the church is a normal condition, and sometimes desirable.

Seminaries now are being urged to train future priests in management techniques and conflict resolution. Certainly this can have an appropriate place, but if it stops there, it is a deadly exercise of Pelagianism. The essential function of the priest in an embattled community is not to resolve all problems, but to interpret for his community what they already know, namely, that the Spirit of God is among them even if they do not recognize it. The priest may be a bungler as far as administrative ability is concerned, but that need not block his essential function as an interpreter of the presence of God among his community.

In all of this, the priest must have the sensitivity for leadership, the charism. However, the ability to act in the name of the community comes from an office bestowed from Someone on high. As the ancient spiritual tradition has it, priestly office is not bestowed because the individual has desired and chosen it, nor because he or anyone else has a right to it. It is one of the paradoxes that charism and office go together, although they appear to be disparate and sometimes in opposition.

It is such realities in the church of today that force us back into the acceptance of conflicting images and the admission of powerlessness. It is simply not playing percentage baseball to think that after twenty centuries we are going to have a neat, logical victory for one side or the other. Nor are we going to have a practical victory if one side uses dominative power and the other public-opinion power. The contention here is that neither is the way to handle the situation. The individual priest will need to choose the image within which he will operate in each particular instance. The church will need to accept a plurality of images. But this is not the end. Such acceptance forces us to return to seeking a new dynamic behind the alternatives. It can most often be validated simply by experience, not by logic. "If you haven't done it, it can't be explained." This is not a relapse into terminal subjectivism or pietism or quietism; it is simply the acceptance of the fact that the world is a mysterious place and the mystery is not that it is not logically explicable, but that it works on a dynamic that logic cannot control.

3. The Paradoxes of the Priesthood

The situation of the priesthood in the United States at present is paradoxical but certainly not terminal. The real crises the priesthood has experienced in our history have not come from the rough and tumble of ordinary life, when people were trying to do the best they could, but through a degeneracy from within. Oversuccess and overachievement have led priests in the past into elitism, luxury, dominance, self-serving power and influence. These have been the corruptions. It is hardly true of the American presbyterate today. The privileges have been picayune, the luxuries have not been outside the reach of average Americans, the scandals of non-celibate living have been relatively mild, the power has been used mostly for the good of others. The essential corruptor of virtue, the achievement of power, does not play the preeminent role in the current problems. In the earlier centuries of the republic, the Catholic priesthood was often a social escalator; the escalator has stopped and we are having to run up the stairs today.

The paradox is that we have talked ourselves into a crisis without any valid reason for doing so. Andrew Greeley has remarked: "The laity are not about to leave the church. The clergy, however, are in the process of committing collective suicide because they do not have enough confidence in themselves and their work to actively recruit young men to follow them into the priesthood."[3] Liberal idealism seems to have turned into its own worst enemy. Most of the changes that have occurred up to the present have been brought about by priests themselves. Unfortunately, they sometimes seem to have relinquished a confident image of priesthood without seeing the responsibilities that freedom entails.

Yet out of all this one must conclude that something good is emerging. Perhaps the real problem of America itself is that we are too successful. At least we seem to think we are. The most secure prophecy would be that a change is in the wind and it is not a favorable wind. Are we being prepared, toughened, fire-tried, for what lies ahead? Certainly our most pressing need is for priests to assume leadership in that invisible world of the spirit. It is not an easy world to live with. It is an immensely challenging and satisfying world to aspire to.

Karl Rahner once wrote about God communicating himself in history:

> It is still a history that seems to man a growing chaos—an impenetrable maze of sin and holiness, light and darkness; a history of simultaneous ascents and downfalls, of blood and tears, of noble achievements and rash presumption; a history that is appalling and magnificent, an ooze of endless trivia and yet a high drama; a history in which the individual is freed from the degradation of self-alienation and is reduced to the status of total insignificance among the billions of his fellow men; a history of arrogant might and the inexorable demands of "planning," yet increasingly unpredictable, with a growing pluralism of cultures, economic systems, political systems; an ever more variegated human consciousness, and a trend toward a society of the masses; so that this pluralism, with all the schizophrenia it begets in the consciousness of the individual, is compressed into a highly inflammable density by a human history ever more closely knit, ever more one.
>
> In the midst of all this history, at a thousand different times and places, in a thousand forms, the one thing occurs which produces and sustains it all: the silent coming of God. This can happen. But whether it really does, and where, is the unfathomable secret of God, and of man's fundamental freedom.[4]

Although Rahner was talking of the role of the bishop, the foregoing is also the priest's function and essence. The priest interprets the silent coming of God. He interprets it not as an individual, but as a leader of the faith community. Where others see the sociological or political or psychological or family or personal forces and conflicts at work, he must see with the eyes of faith the presence and activity of God. Presiding at liturgy, preaching the Gospel, leading the community, reconciling people with God and people with people, taking care of the practicalities that make the community function—in whatever he does, the priest is confirming for the community and the world the presence of God in all things. Jeremiah complained:

> *"The priests asked not,*
> *'Where is the LORD?' "*
>   —JEREMIAH 2:8.

Final Note

Priests are not magicians. They may be comedians. I do not say this in levity; comedy is very serious business.

To say that a priest is a comedian is not to denigrate him. Comedy—or its more usual equivalents for theologians, irony and paradox—has been used from Augustine to Niebuhr.[1] Nicholas of Cusa made a whole methodology out of the congruence of opposites. Comedy has its problems as a tool, but it has the great advantage of lying within the province of humble realism.

The priest today needs precisely such a sense. The essential battle is between secularism and spiritual values. Secularism means that we think we live in a self-contained universe that can be explained, controlled and provided for if only we have a little more research and a little more push. Spiritual values mean that there are realities beyond scientific investigation and control. Although doctors can prolong life, they are essentially losers. Only the spiritual person can survive sickness and death.

That is what priests need to remind people of. That is what they need to interpret in the endless flow of secular living. Priests are mystery men.

And then there is another congruence of opposites. For while the priest must stand for spiritual realities or mysteries, he must also be immersed in the daily flow of our earthly life. He cannot stand apart in a pietistic passivism. In the Lord's own words, he must "be in the world, but not of it."

Obviously we have a picture of a man with one foot on earth and the other in heaven. How absurd such a picture really looks, I leave to the reader. But that is exactly the point of the matter. It is absurd. It is not ludicrous; it is simply comic. The priest is like a modern painting that defies the viewer to say which way it should be hung. Perhaps the image means different things in different positions. One thing it does not mean: it is not a commercial illustration.

Thomas Aquinas went a long way toward making religion and life reasonable. It never quite worked out. There is a mystery factor in all lives that sociology and history cannot fathom but can simply record. Story—with its paradoxes and ironies—rather than history or statistics is more accurate as a record of facts.

Priests have been the key storytellers of our civilization. They often see more of life than other people do. They know it from the revelation of people's most serious thoughts and, at times, from the unworldly vistas of eternity with which they are forced to deal. Others may see a story as a tragedy; indeed, tragedy is logic at its saddest, the inevitable destruction of the hero. Some may see it as a series of hero episodes, with either themselves as the hero or with the demand that the hero save them. That also is logical and similar to our demands from government or from education or from business. But the priest, who sees the story from a more-distant viewpoint, knows that it is a comedy.

Such is the Gospel story. It begins with a hero who teaches as no one else ever did and who works wondrous deeds. But then it turns nasty and becomes a tragedy from which the hero cannot escape; it has been decreed. Yet the final word is comic: he is raised from the dead. The conclusion is both illogical and fitting. As long as logic rules the story, we are able to identify ourselves with it. But then the only final way to express God's action in human affairs is through comedy. That makes God present. And in the long run, that is what a priest does in an official and enduring way.

However one wants to describe the image—dispenser of mysteries, sealed with a character, *in persona Christi*, image of Christ the high priest, spiritual shepherd, leader of the community of faith, interpreter of their faith, or comedian—we are always dealing with the same distinctive characteristic. There is a mystery which inhabits these men. We need more of that today. We need priests who are simply the presence of Christ among us. Perhaps we need more priests as comedians in the true sense.

Notes

Chapter Two

1. Cf. Jean Galot, S.J., *Theology of the Priesthood* (San Francisco: Ignatius Press, 1984). This competent but conservative statement was distributed to all U.S. bishops at the expense of the USCB. Edward Schillebeeckx, *The Church with a Human Face* (New York: Crossroad, 1985). Schillebeeckx stresses that his latest approach incorporates a socio-historical viewpoint since theology cannot be expressed in a single dimension or language; cf. pg. 4–5.

2. The bibliography on the historical theology of the priesthood is enormous. I note here only those publications I found of particular importance to this work. Paul J. LeBlanc, "A Survey of Recent Writings on Ministry and Orders," *Worship* 49 (1975), 35–56. This is the most extensive survey in English but needs updating. Angelo Urru, "Recentiora Problemata Circa Sacram Ordinationem," *Angelicum* 57 (1980), 344–72. This has a bibliography of more-recent pontifical documents. Bernard Cooke, *Ministry to Word and Sacraments History and Theology* (Philadelphia: Fortress, 1976), 636–656, "Theological Reflections on Sacramental Ministry." Edward J. Kilmartin, "Office and Charism: Reflections on a New Study of Ministry," *Theological Studies* 38 (1977), is an excellent critique of Cooke. Cf. also: "Apostolic Office: Sacrament of Christ," *Theological Studies* 36 (1975), 243–24. H. Richard Niebuhr, ed., *The Ministry in Historical Perspectives* (San Francisco: Harper & Row, 1981). Thomas J. Green, "The Revision of Canon Law: Theo-

logical Implications," *Theological Studies* 40 (1979), 593–679, has an extensive discussion about clerical authority. Joseph Lecuyer, *Le Sacrament de l'Ordination: Reserche Historiche et Theologique* (Paris: Beauchesne, 1981). Thomas Franklin O'Meara, *Theology of Ministry* (New York: Paulist, 1983). This is probably the best-balanced and most-recent book. Karl Rahner, *The Priesthood* (New York: Seabury, 1973). Vintage Rahner. David N. Power, *Gifts That Differ: Lay Ministries Established and Unestablished* (New York: Pueblo, 1980). Despite the use of the term "lay" in the title, this book has much to say about the historical development of the priesthood and says it well. Preliminary Report of the Systematic Theology Committee on Priesthood, USCB, 1972. mss. This report was never approved by the Bishops' Conference. Jean Galot, *Theology of the Priesthood*, op.cit. Manuel Miguens, *Church Ministries in New Testament Times* (Arlington, Va.: Christian Culture Press, 1976). Edward Schillebeeckx, *Ministry: Leadership in the Community of Jesus Christ* (New York: Crossroads, 1981). Cf. NCCB Committee on Doctrine, Sept. 2, 1983, Letter to Bishops concerning E. Schillebeeckx's book on ministry.

3 John Grindel, "Old Testament and Christian Priesthood," *Communio* 3 (Spring, 1976), 16–38, and Mary Collins in footnote 6 following.

4 *Epistolae S. Aureli Augustini*, XXIII, *Corpus Scriptorum Ecclesiae Latinae*, vol. 34 (Vindobonae: F. Tempsky, 1885), 65, author's translation.

5 Robert M. Grant, *The Apostolic Fathers* (New York: Thomas Nelson, 1964), 169. John Henry Cardinal Newman and H.R. Niebuhr were both aware of the crucial nature of this quick development in church history. Newman virtually made it the basis for his theory of the development of doctrine. The problem is posed in a somewhat different and more theoretical way today. The relationship of charism and office is involved here and it is one of the most difficult questions in speculative theology. Both exist and with tension; the attempts to eliminate the tension end with denying the existence of one or the other. Cf. especially Kilmartin, Cooke and Power. Schillebeeckx, *Face,* from a more historical perspective, is also aware that the step between the first and second centuries is crucial.

6 The early sacramentaries are quite clear on the decisive role of the coming of the Holy Spirit on the ordinand. The election and deputation to cult are clear but do not eliminate the even more important role of the prayer and the imposition of hands. Cf. Mary Collins, "The Public Language of Ministry" in James H. Provost, ed., *Official Ministry in a New Age* (Washington, D.C.). Canon Law Society of America, Permanent Seminar Studies, No. 3, 1981, 7–40. This is an excellent study of the development of the language of the ordination ritual, especially that of Hippolytus, which is the basis for the 1968 revision of the *Pontificale Romanum.* The text reveals a first layer of sacerdotal theocracy that comes from late Judaism; a second layer of hierarchical schemes representing invisible realities on a Platonic and Neoplatonic basis; and, finally, a last layer of organizational wisdom that comes from the public institutions of the Empire, both Roman and Byzantine. The conclusion is rather odd, namely, that the theology of Vatican II testifies to the

malformation of the self-understanding of the church and its structuring.

7 Clement of Rome (circa 95 A.D. at the latest) already uses "laics" to refer to those subject to the authorities in Corinth. The use of the term "clergy" does not appear to antedate Tertullian (circa 160–222 A.D.).

8 Hans Kung, *Why Priests?, A Proposal for a New Church Ministry* (Garden City: Doubleday, 1972), 64, expressed the idea that Augustine tossed off the concept of character in the heat of argument with the Donatists but that there was not much more behind it than a debating point. Schillebeeckx also in *Face*, 142, conveys the same attitude.

Chapter Three

1 Edward Schillebeeckx, *The Church with a Human Face* (New York: Crossroad, 1985), 204–205.

2 "The Ministerial Priesthood; Document of the Third Synod of Bishops, 1971" (Hales Corners, WI: Priests of the Sacred Heart), taken from *L'Osservatore Romano*, Dec. 16, 1971. A fuller compilation of such documents can be found in Odile M. Liebard, *Clergy & Laity* (Wilmington, N.C.: McGrath, 1978), 323.

3 *On Due Process* (Washington, D.C.: NCCB, 1969). This includes both the Report of the Canon Law Society of America to the National Conference of Catholic Bishops on the Subject of Due Process and the NCCB on the Subject of Due Process.

4 Thomas J. Green, "The Revision of Canon Law: Theological Implications," Th St 40 (D 1979), 593–679, cf. 641. The same point was raised by Edward J. Kilmartin, "Office and Charisms: Reflections on a New Study of Ministry." Th St 38 (S 1977), 547–554, from a theological viewpoint.

5 Study on Priestly Life and Ministry, Summaries of the Report of the Ad Hoc Bishops' Subcommittees on History, Sociology and Psychology, NCCB (Washington, D.C., 1971).

6 Report of the Subcommittee on the Systematic Theology of the Priesthood of the NCCB's Committee on Priestly Life and Ministry; Carl J. Armbruster, John J. Begley, Walter J. Burghardt, Avery R. Dulles, Michael A. Fahey, Richard P. McBrien, Reginald Masterson, Ladislas M. Orsy, Anthony T. Padovano. As far as I know, this exists only in mimeographed form.

7 Sacred Congregation for the Faith Declaration on the Question of the Ordination of Women to the Ministerial Priesthood, October 15, 1976. Cf. Odile Leibard, op. cit., 374–389.

8 *As One Who Serves*, Bishops' Committee on Priestly Life and Ministry (Washington, D.C.: USCC, 1977).

9 Robert K. Greenleaf, *Servant Leadership* (New York: Paulist, 1977).

10 Andrew Greeley, ed., *The Catholic Priest in the United States: Sociological Investigations* (Washington, D.C.: USCC, 1972); referred to as NORC since the survey was conducted by the National Opinion Research Center. Eugene F. Hemrick and Dean R. Hoge, *Seminarians in Theology: A National Profile* (Washington, D.C.: USCC, 1985). Dean R. Hoge,

Raymond H. Potin, Kathleen M. Ferry, *Research on Men's Vocations to the Priesthood and the Religious Life* (Washington, D.C.: United States Catholic Conference, 1984).

11 Schillebeeckx, *Face*, cf. 203–208 for his best summary.

12 Bernard Cooke, *Ministry to Word and Sacraments: History and Theology* (Philadelphia: Fortress, 1976). Cooke describes the priestly character of the church and then identifies the ministerial priesthood as a "specific directedness to some function that enables the community to express its priestly character" (644). Cf. also O'Meara, Power, the preliminary report of the NCCB Subcommittee, among others, which is mainly on the conventional side and yet reaches radical practical conclusions or at least makes suggestions about permanence, celibacy, male-only ordination.

13 Cooke, *Ministry*, 644. Cooke understands charism and office (i.e., the ministerial priesthood in this case) as being inevitably in tension. In a later book, *Sacraments and Sacramentality* (Mystic, Ct.: Cook, 1983), Cooke considerably downplayed the tension in favor of the common ministry of the baptized.

14 Jean Galot, S.J., *Theology of the Priesthood* (San Francisco: Ignatius Press, 1984). This book was sent to all bishops and rectors of seminaries by courtesy of NCCB. For reference to Roman documents, cf. Liebard, supra.

15 Cf. Cooke, *Ministry*. Thomas F. O'Meara, *Theology of Ministry* (New York: Paulist, 1983).

16 Cooke, *Ministry*, 644.

17 Dennis Geany and John Ring, *What a Modern Catholic Believes About Priesthood* (Chicago: Thomas More, 1971). Probably represents an extreme view on professionalism in the immediate wake of Vatican II.

18 Robert J. Schreiter, "What Cultural Influences Have an Effect Upon the Ecclesiologies Current in the United States?" Seminaries in Dialogue, NCEA, 10 (May, 1985), 12–20.

19 David J. OBrien, "The American Priest and Social Action," in *The Catholic Priest in the United States* (Collegeville, Minn.: St. John's University Press, 1971), esp. pp. 448 ff.

20 Martin Marty, *The Public Church* (Crossroad: New York, 1981), Chapter 1 especially.

21 Henrick-Hoge, *Seminarians*, 26–29.

22 Austin Flannery, *Vatican Council II* (Collegeville, Minn.: The Liturgical Press, 1975), Dogmatic Constitution on the Church, # 12, 363. "The whole body of the faithful who have an anointing that comes from the holy one cannot err in matters of belief."

23 James Provost, "Renewed Canonical Understanding of Official Ministry" in *Official Ministry in the Church* (CLSA Permanent Seminar Studies, No. 3, Washington, D.C.: CSLA, 1981). Cf. also Green and Kilmartin in footnote 4.

24 Andrew Greeley, *Sociological Investigations*, 314.

25 Andrew Greeley, *American Catholics Since the Council: An Unauthorized Report* (Chicago: Thomas More Press, 1985), 122.

26 Greeley, *Sociological Investigations,* 127–128.

27 Greeley, *Sociological Investigations,* 270–271.

28 John Tracy Ellis, "The Formation of the American Priest: An Historical Perspective," in *The Catholic Priest in the United States, Historical Investigations* (Collegeville, Minn.: St. John's University Press, 1971), 111–292.

29 Susan Schnur, a rabbi and religion teacher at Colgate University, reviewed Rosemary Reuther's book, *Women-Church,* in the New York Times Book Review, Dec. 21, 1986, and remarked: "One measure of Catholic feminists' fierce debarment from the church actually can be inferred from how old-fashioned Ms. Reuther's feminism is. . . . Where else in this country, in this era of assimilation, is feminism still reactive, angry, full of revolutionary intellectual brimstone?"

30 The Bishops' Committee on Priestly Life and Ministry, *The Priest and Stress* (Washington, D.C.: USCC, 1982), Outline.

31 Greeley, *Sociological Investigations,* summary pp. 311–316.

Chapter Four

1 Eugene F. Hemrick and Dean R. Hoge, *Seminarians in Theology: A National Profile* (Washington, D.C.: USCC, 1985), referred to as *Seminarians.* The National Task Force Report on the Fiscal Resources of Catholic Theology Schools, 1975–1983, *Planning the Future* (Washington, D.C.: Center for Applied Research in the Apostolate, May, 1980), referred to as the CARA-Lilly Study. William Cardinal Baum, Sacred Congregation for Catholic Education, Letter to the Cardinals, Archbishops and Bishops of the Church in the United States of America, Prot. N 982/80, 14th September, 1985, referred to as Letter of Sacred Congregation.

2 *Seminarians,* 11–13 for data in this paragraph.

3 CARA-Lilly, 8. In May, 1980, the projection of costs for 1983 was $17.000 per year.

4 *Seminarians,* 13.

5 *Seminarians,* 2, #23.

6 Letter of Sacred Congregation, 17. "Sometimes the psychological and sociological dimensions of problem-solving can obscure the specifically priestly dimension."

7 *Seminarians,* pg. 2, #21.

8 There is no published data on this but I know from the personal experience of talking to bishops and prominent seminary administrators that this is a known analysis of the situation.

9 *Seminarians,* 1, #2.

10 *Seminarians,* 1, #7.

11 *Seminarians,* 2, #29.

[12] *Seminarians*, 1, #3.

[13] *Seminarians*, 1, #11–12.

[14] *Seminarians*, 2, #16.

[15] *Seminarians*, 3, #36.

[16] *Seminarians*, 2, #25.

[17] *Seminarians*, 46.

[18] CARA-Lilly, 8. "Ordinaries (episcopal and religious) sending their personnel to seminaries they do not own and operate should realize their obligation in justice to pay a larger amount of the per-student costs over and above tuition and room and board than is the common practice today."

[19] Bishops' Committee on Priestly Formation, *Program of Priestly Formation* (Washington, D.C.: NCCB).

[20] Letter of Sacred Congregation, passim.

[21] Letter of Sacred Congregation, 3.

[22] Seminaries in Dialogue, 9 (May, 1985), 8.

[23] NCEA Seminary News, 23 (Dec. 1984), 5. "After registering an increase in enrollment during the past two years, the seminary theologates declined in priesthood enrollment from 4,244 in 1983–84 to 4,170 in 1984–85. The present enrollment, however is still superior to the 1982–83 figure of 3,819."

[24] Andrew M. Greeley, *American Catholics Since the Council* (Chicago: Thomas More, 1985), 127. "What has gone wrong in the Catholic priesthood in the United States since the Second Vatican Council? Even stated as simply as that last question, the crisis in the priesthood remains to a considerable extent inexplicable. The changes of the Second Vatican Council did something to the priesthood from which it has yet to recover. Until we understand better than we do now why the Council was such a savage blow to the morale, the self-esteem, the self-confidence and the self-respect of priests, we will have to accept as almost inevitable the continued decline in the number of priests available to minister to the church and the mounting problems for laity and for priests because of that decline."

[25] *Seminarians*, 47.

Chapter Five

[1] Ernest E. Larkin and Gerard T. Broccolo, eds., *Spiritual Renewal of the American Priesthood* (Washington, D.C.: USCC, 1973), and *As One Who Serves*, Bishops' Committee on Priestly Life and Ministry (Washington, D.C.: USCC, 1977).

[2] Eugene Walsh, *The Priesthood in the Writings of the French School* (Washington, D.C.: Catholic University, 1949), 6, 14.

[3] Cf. such novels as Bruce Marshall's *The World, the Flesh, and Father Smith* and *Father Malachy's Miracle*; Henry Robinson's *The Cardinal*; A.J. Cronin's *Keys of the Kingdom*; Graham Greene's *Labyrinthian Ways*, and others too numerous to be mentioned or too insignificant to be

noted. Cf. Michael Pfliegher, *Priestly Existence* (Westminster: Newman, 1957); Leonard Fick, "An Appraisal: The Priest in Contemporary American Fiction," Journal of Theology (Fall/Winter), 1984. Many motion pictures have featured priests; e.g. Spencer Tracy in "Boys' Town", Gregory Peck in "The Keys of the Kingdom", Frank Sinatra in "Miracle of the Bells", Montgomery Clift in "I Confess", Don Murray in "The Hoodlum Priest", Ward Bond in "The Quiet Man", Rex Harrison in "The Agony and the Ecstasy", Tom Tryon and John Huston in "The Cardinal", Sean Connery in "The Name of the Rose", Jack Lemmon in "Mass Appeal", Milo O'Shea in "The Verdict" and Karl Malden in "On the Waterfront". A recent article by Budd Schulberg in the New York Times Book Reviews (April 26, 1987) recalled the real life Fr. John Corridan who was the inspiration for the book from which "On the Waterfront" was made. Besides this there were such TV series as Richard Chamberlain in "The Thorn Birds", Robert Blake in "Helltown" and Tommy Lee Jones in "Broken Vows", etc. Obviously the subject of priests is fascinating to the media.

4 "Decree on the Life and Ministry of Priests," Dec. 7, 1965.

5 Cf. footnote 1 above.

6 Joseph M. White, "American Diocesan Seminaries, 1791 to the 1980s," Seminaries in Dialogue, 13 (Apr. 1986), 16–19.

7 Cf. John Tracy Ellis, "The Formation of the American Priest: An Historical Perspective" in *The Catholic Priest in the United States, Historical Investigations* (NORC, Collegeville, Minn.: St. John's Abbey Press, 1971), and the small summary entitled, "Report of the Subcommittee on History" in *Study on Priestly Life and Ministry* (Washington, D.C.: NCCB, 1971). Ellis takes a most dismal view of the intellectual training of American priests before 1960. He is also highly critical of the failure to establish a central U.S. seminary, presumably at Catholic University of America. Oddly enough, Ellis seems to take a rather benign view of the present training of priests except for the plurality of seminaries. A much better-balanced although brief viewpoint can be found in Robert J. Schreiter, "Fragmentation and Unity in Theological Education," Seminaries in Dialogue, NCEA, 10 (1985, May), 2–11.

8 Cf. Letter of William Cardinal Baum, 14 Sept. 1986. Prot. N. 982/80.

9 Cf. Jacques Delarue, *The Missionary Ideal of the Priesthood*, in-house publication, St. Louis: Vincentian Fathers and Brothers (1984), 127.

10 Delarue, 125.

11 Delarue, 121.

12 The Congregation of the Mission and the Daughters of Charity in the United States jointly sponsor the publication, "Vincentian Heritage." An international critical edition of St. Vincent's works is presently in publication. The 72nd national meeting of leaders of St. Vincent de Paul Societies at Notre Dame University in 1986 drew many hundreds of participants. The Catholic Charities organizations in the United States draw their origin and inspiration from the St. Vincent de Paul Society.

13 Delarue, 36.

14 Delarue, 36–37.

[15] Delarue, 40.
[16] Delarue, 27.
[17] Delarue, 54.

Chapter Six

[1] Cf. John Grindel, "Old Testament and Christian Priesthood," *Communio* 3 (1976), 16–38.

[2] Austin Flannery, *Vatican Council II* (Collegeville, Minn.: Liturgical Press, 1975), *Lumen Gentium* 35, pg. 392.

[3] Cf. Flannery, "Decree on Ministry and Life of Priests," #2, pg. 864.

[4] Cf. Flannery, "Decree on the Apostolate of Lay People," #2, pg. 768. The Council also noted anent our point: "The lay apostolate allows of different kinds of relations with the hierarchy, depending on the various forms and objects of this apostolate. In the Church are to be found, in fact, very many apostolic enterprises owing their origin to the free choice of the laity and run at their own discretion. . . . But no enterprise must lay claim to the name 'Catholic' if it has not the approval of legitimate ecclesiastical authority." #24.

[5] Statement of the Board of Directors of CTSA submitted to the Inquiry Committee of the Academic Senate at the Catholic University of America. Testimony regarding the case of Rev. Dr. Charles Curran, under cover of letter of Monika Hellwig, President, Dec. 4, 1986.

[6] Cf. Statement of CTSA under "Institutional."

[7] Cf. John Meier, New York Times Book Review, Dec. 21, 1986, for a well-nuanced statement of the limitations on what the historical authenticity of the life of Jesus can mean for a Catholic who also has tradition and church teaching to guide the conclusions.

[8] Andrew Greeley, *American Catholics Since the Council* (Chicago: Thomas More, 1985). In his introduction, Greeley has a very commonsense declaration about the limitations of sociology as a determinant of theological truth.

[9] In the 1985 Catholic Directory, Chicago is listed as having some 64 subdepartments under 6 major divisions; 25 years ago it had 22. New York has 69 Offices and Directors now; 25 years ago it had 39; Los Angeles numbers 51 now and 35 then. New Ulm, Minn., has 40 now, 15 then. Seattle 20 and 53; Peoria 20 and 34. The growth factor has been multiform; Catholic Charities has expanded into all sorts of specialized services, and then there are offices for cursillo, marriage encounter, family counseling, youth ministry. The clergy account for a part of the growth: Priests' Senate, personnel, retirement. Finance has become more sophisticated, including data processing, pension funds, planning. One can sometimes pick up a sense of problems now as then in such titles as "Pastoral Ministry with Refugees," "Pastoral Outreach to the Chinese," "Indian Ministry"; one could do that 25 years ago with "Offices for Literature" and a "Bishops' School Bus Commission." The point here is not to criticize dioceses for doing things that are Christian and needed; it is simply to show that chancery offices are a growth

industry and that like any bureaucracy, they seem to spread out and perpetuate themselves without regard to the ideology that gave rise to them.

10 The precise definition of what are "official" organizations under the hierarchy and what are quasi-independent lay activities is still not clear. Vatican II, "Lay People," #22, noted with approval the different kinds of relationships of lay groups to the hierarchy. Vatican II, *Ad Gentes*, #21, spoke of the "laity existing and working alongside the hierarchy." Before Vatican II, the usual formula for the lay apostolate was "the participation of the laity in the apostolate of the hierarchy." The new formula for the laity seems to be the apostolate of inserting the Gospel as a leaven into the reality of the world in which the laity live and work. Cf. Leonard Doohan, *John Paul II and the Laity* (Le Jacq Publishing, Inc., 1984) 8, for Pope John Paul II's. The Fourth General Assembly of the Synod of Bishops, 1977, had much to say on this subject. Cf. *The Synod, The Laity, and Catechesis* (Vatican City, The Laity Today, 1978). An aspect of this is the felt danger of "basic communities" that might become too independent; that aspect came up often enough in the debates, without a final solution. In actual American practice, we have had many organizations of Catholics with only a vague dependence on the hierarchy. The *Catholic Almanac* (Huntington, Ind.: Our Sunday Visitor Press) usually has about 8 pages of listings (some 200 entries) of associations, movements, societies. Some of these are professional, some pious and some special-action groups, including insurance groups. They vary from the Calix Society, which helps Catholic alcoholics, to the Slovak Catholic Sokol. The fifties and sixties saw much involvement by Catholics in social causes, from Dorothy Day's "Catholic Worker" to participation in Saul Alinsky's Back of the Yards Movement in Chicago. The umbrella groups are the National Council of Catholic Men, National Council of Catholic Women, and the National Council of Catholic Laity.

11 Andrew Greeley, *American Catholics*, 49–79, summarizes the research thus: "Beginning in 1969, this proportion of Sunday Mass attendance (66% each Sunday: ed. note from preceding sentence) began to decline precipitously. By 1975, the proportion of Catholics attending Mass every week hovered around 50%. . . . The decline stopped in 1975 as suddenly as it had started 6 years before" (pp. 54–55). Then Greeley points out that it leveled off at 10% above Protestant Church attendance, a figure virtually constant since 1940. He attributes this from a sociological model off which he worked to the "one jolt" shock of *Humanae Vitae* and the recovery to dissident Catholics finding a way to reconcile their dissidence on this teaching with acceptance through an image of a loving God. In effect, however, the extremely tenacious loyalty to religious faith as a whole has won out. As Greeley remarks elsewhere, the faithful are not about to leave the church even when they disagree with it.

Chapter Seven

1 The final argument here is based upon the thesis set forth in Robert J.

Daly, ed., *Christian Biblical Ethics* (New York: Paulist Press, 1984), which was a production of a continuing seminar of the Catholic Biblical Association.

[2] For an excellent treatment on paradox as an operating principle in life, cf. Charles L. Whitfield, M.D., "Stress Management and Spirituality during Recovery: A Transpersonal Approach," in *Alcoholism Treatment Quarterly*, 1 (Summer, 1984), 1–50. Joseph Ratzinger in a 1971 pamphlet, "Priestly Ministry: A Search for its Meaning" (New York: Sentinel Press, 1971), makes the same point about images and has a good explanation of the Hebrews' image. He is also aware that the warring factions in 1971 were fighting the battle of whether we should change or stay with what we have.

[3] Andrew Greeley, *American Catholics Since the Council* (Chicago: Thomas More, 1985), 122. As a sociologist, he finds the situation inexplicable.

[4] Karl Rahner, *Servants of the Lord* (New York: Herder and Herder, 1968), 19–20.

Index

A

Abolition of mandatory celibacy
  often proposed, 68, 75
Ad Gentes
  Vatican II, 189
American Priest
  images of, 129–30
Apostolate of Lay People
  Vatican II, 155
Apostolic
  Quality of teacher, 172
Aquinas, Thomas
  on character, 51
  reasonable view of life, 178
  story, 46–50
Areas of life
  for priests and laity, 83–
    84
As One Who Serves

Bishops' statement on priesthood, 67, 183
Augustine
  City of God, 45, 170
  on character, 42, 43, 46, 51
  story, 38–43
Authority
  used by Paul at Corinth, 26–
    27
  primary problem in research
    reports, 67

B

Baptism
  cannot be lost, 45–46
Bishop
  as used in New Testament,
    29

Bishops
  presiding with presbyterate,
    44
Borromeo, Charles
  story, 54–57
Brown, Peter
  Augustine of Hippo, 42

C

Canon Law Society of America
  criticism of new Code, 65–
    66
  letter on C. Curran, 158–59
  On Due Process, 183
CARA-Lilly Study
  Planning the Future, 113,
    115, 185, 186
Catholic
  first used by Ignatius, 36
Catholic Almanac
  listing of lay organizations,
    189
Catholic Directory
  on chancery offices, 188–
    89
Catholics
  accepted into mainstream
    America, 82
Celibacy (cf. Mandatory celi-
    bacy)
  no great significance, 75
  priests' opinion, 91
Changes of Vatican II
  and societal changes, 84
  essential or cosmetic, 63
  relatively slight concerning
    priests, 64
Changes in seminaries
  statistics, 107–08
Character

arguments concerning nature,
    72
  as "relatedness", 73
  at Trent, 59, 74
  Augustine and, 42, 43, 46, 51
  conventional view (ontologi-
    cal), 72
  crucial problem, 68
  in medieval universities, 53
  in Thomas Aquinas, 51
  nature not defined at Trent,
    59
  "sphargis" permanent, 46
Charisms and office
  distinction and connection, 71
Christ the Priest
  French spirituality, 59
Churches in America
  role in public life, 81–82
Civil religion
  struggle to control, 83
Clergy
  personal or communitarian,
    73–74
  separate from laity in Igna-
    tius, 37
Clergy and laity
  separate spheres, 156
Clerical ghetto
  abandoned, 83
Code of Canon Law, 1983
  new vision of ministry, 65
  on priests and People of God,
    65
  "sacred ministers", 65
Collegiality
  Vatican II concept, 162–63
Collins, Mary
  "The Public Language of Min-
    istry", 182
Comedian
  priest as comedian, 177

Comedy
  as interpretation of life, 178
Common priesthood
  Vatican II, 154
Conflict
  of images, 63
  of opinions about Vatican II,
    63
Conflict resolution
  training in, 173
Conzelmann, Hans
  1 Corinthians, 25
Cooke, Bernard
  Ministry, 181, 184
  on priestly character, 73
  Sacraments and Sacramental-
    ity, 184
Corporation
  realistic model of church, 161
  tendency of church to be-
    come, 85
Cosmic event
  priests make God present, 170
Coste, Pierre
  Life of St. Vincent de Paul,
    138
  Conferences of St. Vincent,
    138
Council of Trent
  decrees on sacraments, 59
  opposition to decrees, 58
  reinstituted seminaries, 57
  decrees on priesthood, 17
Crisis in priesthood
  without valid reason, 174

D

Daly, Robert J.
  Christian Biblical Ethics,
    189–90

Deacon
  clearly defined in New Testa-
    ment, 29
Delarue, Jacques
  Ideal of Priesthood, 138,
    187–88
Democratic procedures
  in American Catholic church,
    163
Dependence on God
  Vincent de Paul on, 144
Differences—priests and
    bishops
  on all issues, 93–94
  social attitudes, 91
Dignity of human beings
  in Vincentian spirituality,
    147
Diocesan Chancery Offices
  expansion, 160
Doohan, Leonard
  John Paul II and the Laity,
    189
Douglass, H. Paul
  The St. Louis Church Survey,
    79

E

Ecclesiastical structure
  dissatisfaction with, 93
Ecclesiology
  at heart of priesthood prob-
    lem, 69
Equality of baptized
  crucial problem, 68
  proposed by Schillebeeckx,
    70
Ellis, John Tracy
  Historical Investigations, 185,
    187

Empower
  within church structure, 159
Enthusiasm
  in church at Corinth, 26
Ethnic priest
  Fr. Tim Dempsey, 76–79
  church as escalator for immi-
    grants, 79
Eucharist
  center of priest's actions, 51–
    52

F

Father Smith
  story, 1–15
Flannery, Austin
  Vatican Council II, 184, 188
Formation
  changes in seminaries, 110
Fourth Roman Synod
  on the role of the laity, 189
Freedom
  in church at Corinth, 26
French School
  centered on Christ the Priest,
    59
Function and nature of priest-
    hood
  expressed in images, 16

G

Galot, Jean
  Theology of the Priesthood,
    181, 184
  his story, 21
Geany-Ring
  What a Modern Catholic Be-
    lieves about Priesthood,
    184

Gilby, Thomas
  Political Thought of Thomas
    Aquinas, 50
Going My Way
  no longer current standard,
    16
  outdated but evocative, 84
  scene from, 9
Grant, Robert M.
  The Apostolic Fathers, 35,
    182
Greeley, Andrew
  American Catholics, 91, 174,
    185, 186, 189
  Ascent Into Hell, 15
  The Catholic Priest (NORC),
    90, 183, 184, 185
Green, Thomas J.
  criticism of new Code, 65–
    66
  fundamental Christian equal-
    ity, 65
  "The Revision of Canon
    Law", 181–82
Greene, Graham
  The Power and the Glory, 7,
    16
  Whiskey Priest, 7
Grindel, John
  Old Testament Priesthood,
    182, 188

H

Hemrick-Hoge
  Seminarians in Theology,
    104–05, 183
Hero stories
  as interpretation of life, 178
Hierarchy
  conventional thesis of, 70–71
  in Ignatius, 37

High Priest
   entering Holy of Holies, 167
Historical development
   argument from, 69–70
Hoge, Potvin, Ferry
   Research on Men's Vocations,
    183–84
Holiness
   demand for in seminaries,
    118
Humanae Vitae
   shock of on priesthood, 189
Humility and obedience
   needed in priesthood, 146–
    47

I

Ignatius
   story, 29–34
Images
   priests and People of God,
    64
   conflict in priests, 168
   determine theology, 168
   in definition of priest, 16
   used by Ignatius, 36
   Vatican II and images, 63
Infallibility
   in the community, 84, 184
Instrument
   priest as, 138, 148

J

Jesuits
   in American seminaries, 130
Jesus
   as rabbi with learners, 27
Johnston, James E.

"Priests, Prose and Preachment", 16
Judaism
   institutional priesthood, 152

K

Kilmartin, Edward
   "Apostolic Office", 181
   "Office and Charism", 181
Kleist, James
   Ancient Christian Writers,
    34
Kung, Hans
   Why Priests?, 183

L

Laics and clerics
   in Clement of Rome, 183
Laity
   and crisis in priesthood, 93
   apostolate, 155
   Fourth Roman Synod, 189
   involvement in ministry, 162
   not about to leave church, 93
   secular evangelization, 156–
    57
Larkin-Broccolo
   Spiritual Renewal of Priest-
    hood, 186
Lay ministry
   cultic functions, 160
Lay organizations
   decrease in number, 161
Lay theologians
   education, 156
   obligation of communion,
    159
Leadership
   charism in priest, 173

LeBlanc, Paul J.
  "A Survey of Recent Writ-
    ings", 181
Lecuyer, Joseph
  Le Sacrament de l'Ordination,
    182
Letter of Cardinal Baum
  Vatican visitation of seminar-
    ies, 114, 115–16, 131,
    185, 186
Liberal attitudes
  of priests, 91
Life and Ministry of Priests
  common priesthood, 154–55
Liturgy
  Paul's control over, 25, 27
  purposes, 171
Lumen Gentium
  on common priesthood, 154

M

Mainstream America
  Catholics join, 82
Management techniques
  training in, 173
Mandatory celibacy
  priests' attitude toward, 91
Marty, Martin
  The Public Church, 184
McAuliffe, Harold
  Father Tim, 79
Meier, John
  Historical Jesus, 188
Miguens, Manuel
  Church Ministries, 35, 182
Minister
  in Protestant Reformation, 52
Ministerial priesthood
  not the same as professional-
    ism, 17

Ministry
  professional, 157
  within Church structures, 157
Monarchial episcopacy
  among the Fathers, 44
Mystery
  in church ministry, 174
  in the church, 170
  priests as mystery men, 178
Mystique of priesthood
  among seminarians, 112

N

Nicholas of Cusa
  Congruence of Opposites,
    177
Niebuhr, Richard H.
  The Ministry, 181
NORC (cf. also Greeley)
  The Catholic Priest, 67, 90,
    91, 92, 93, 94, 97, 183

O

O'Brien, David J.
  Priest and Social Action, 184
O'Meara, Thomas Franklin
  Theology of Ministry, 72,
    182
Obediential potency
  in Thomas Aquinas, 51
Old Boys' Network
  way of operating, 94
Order
  in medieval times, 53
Ordinary power
  in new Code of Canon Law,
    65
  need for, 85

practical problems, 67–68
Thomas Aquinas' problem, 68
Ordination ritual
early sacramentaries, 44
Organization
in New Testament, 28
Orr, William F.
1 Corinthians, 25

P

Paradox
function of, 169
of church's existence, 169
of essential church teachings, 169
of priestly office, 170
Paradoxes
of priesthood, 174
Parish ministries
recent expansion, 161
Perseverence
in priesthood, 74–75
Paul
story, 22–25
Pontificale Romanum
1968 use of Hippolytus, 182
Power
of order, 51, 53
Power, David N.
Gifts that Differ, 182
Powerlessness
to control church affairs, 173–74
Presbyterate
permanent, 73–74
early church, 44
Presbyters
council of, 44
Presbytery
in Ignatius, 37

Priest
"absolute" forbidden, 45
acting out public image, 168
as used in New Testament, 29
as man of action, 81
as professional minister, 75
differences from lay, 75
Paul as priest, 25
representative of presbyterate, 171
social action, 82–83
Priest—Christian
early tradition, 153
Priest and Stress
Bishops' Committee Report, 96, 185
Priest and theologian
distinction between, 158–59
Priest as teacher
in early tradition, 153–54
Malachi 2:7, 152
Priesthood
Bishops' study of, 66
Priestly Life and Ministry
Bishops' Committee Report, 183
Priestly office
paradoxical nature, 170
Priests
as story-tellers, 178
emotional maturity, 91
distinctive characteristic, 179
liberal or conservative?, 91
non-priestly professions, 161
Priests and Bishops
historical relations in U.S., 94
Priests and Stress
Bishops' Committee report, 96–97
Priests' Senates
problems, 94

Provost, James
  Official Ministry, 184

R

Rahner, Karl
  Servants of the Lord, 190
  The Priesthood, 182
  the silent coming of God,
    175
Ratzinger, Joseph
  Priestly Ministry, 190
Reconciliation
  office of reconciler, 172–73
Redemption
  as portrayed in New Testa-
    ment, 28
Reformation
  accomplishments, 58–59
  and priesthood, 57
  causes, 57
Religious experience
  factor in perseverence, 92
Reordination of priests
  Trent, 57
Roman Synod
  on laity, 189
  on priests, 64–65
  The Ministerial Priesthood,
    183
Rothensteiner, John
  History of Archdiocese of St.
    Louis, 79
Royal Priesthood
  1 Peter 2:9, 151, 152–53
  Exodus 19:4–6, 151–52

S

Sacrament
  in Augustine, 43

Sacred ministers
  in Code of Canon Law, 65
Sacred ministers and People of
    God
  in new Code of Canon Law,
    65
Sacrifice
  and priest, 153
Schillebeeckx, Edward
  equality of all the baptized,
    70
  Ministry, 182
  story, 21
  The Church with a Human
    Face, 181, 183
Schnur, Susan
  review of Women-Church,
    185
Schreiter, Robert J.
  Cultural Influences, 184
Seminarians
  attitudes today, 105
Seminarians in Theology
  conclusions, 105
  future seminarians, 117–18
  source of Joe Seminarian
    story, 104–05
Seminarians of the Sixties
  1966–67 Study, 105
Seminaries
  academics, 109
  changes since Vatican II, 131
  commonalities, 114
  continued characteristics, 112
  early American, 128
  faculty, 116–17
  finances, 108, 185
  future influences on, 117–18
  lack of a national policy, 113
  volunteer networking, 114–15
Seminary education
  largely practical, 145
Silence

the silent coming of God, 175
Social justice
and contemporary seminari-
ans, 106, 112
Spiritual Renewal of Priesthood
Bishops' Statement, 127–28
Spirituality
American Bishops, 127–28
French School, 126
history, 124
of American seminaries, 128
popular novels, 126
practical, 124
Vatican II, 126–27
Story
use of vignettes, xx
Stress
among priests, 96–97
Subcommittee on Systematic
Theology
report unpublished, 66, 182,
183
Subsidiarity
Vatican II concept, 162–63
Sulpicians
in the United States, 60

T

Teaching Sisters
role in educating immigrants,
81
Temporary priestly service
proposed, 68
Theology and story
in historical theology, 21
Thompson, E. H.
The Prince of Pastors, 57
Thurston, Herbert
St. Charles Borromeo, 57
Tragedy

as interpretation of life, 178–
79
Trisco, Robert
Historical Investigations, 94
Two Swords
political theory, 53

U

Urru, Angelo
"Recentiora Problemata Circa
Sacram Ordinationem",
181

V

Vatican Commission on Seminaries
results of visitations, 114,
115, 116, 131, 185, 187
Vatican II
documents of, 154–55
Constitution on the Church
(Lumen Gentium), 64, 154,
188
Laity, 155, 189
Ministry and Life of Priests,
64, 126–27, 188
Vincent de Paul
and Trent, 59
conducting seminaries, 139
dignity of priesthood, 141
idea of priestly vocation,
139–40
mission, 126
practical need for today, 148
relations with laity, 140–41
Vincentian Heritage
Journal, 187
Vincentians
in the United States, 60

Vocation crisis
  extent and causes, 96
Vocation Directors
  problems, 113
Vocations
  and seminaries, 117
  felt need for among priests, 96
  lack of encouragement, 93
  recruiting, 174

W

Walsh, Eugene
  French School of Spirituality,
    186
Walther, James Arthur
  1 Corinthians, 25

Walz, Angelus
  Saint Thomas Aquinas, 50
White, Joseph M.
  American Diocesan Seminar-
    ies, 187
Whitfield, Charles L.
  Stress Management and Spir-
    ituality, 190
Women's Ordination
  arguments for, 75
  Declaration of Sacred Con-
    gregation, 66–67, 183

Y

Yeo, Margaret
  The Prince of Pastors, 57